Unlocking
The Healing
Power of Pets

Unlocking
The Healing
Power of Pets

What Pets Can Tell You About Your Soul

BY

KURT GASSNER

My-mindguide.com

Unlocking The Healing Power of Pets
Kurt Gassner

Impressum
My-mindguide – The publishing trademarke of trendguide Capital
GmbH, Klenzestr. 42a, 80469 Munich, Germany.

Reg. Nr. HRB Munich 206639, VAT 152 123 159, CEO:
Kurt Friedrich Gassner
Web: www.my-mindguide.com, mail: gassner@my-mindguide.com

Paperback ISBN: 978-3-949978-84-5
Hardback ISBN: 978-3-949978-85-2

Table of Contents

FORWARD

WHY I CAME UP WITH THIS TOPIC...

I became interested in this topic because of my sister, whose story you can read in this book, and my studies of the healing power of hypnotherapies, meditation, and psychology. I fully understand that this is a way of healing, and horses have played a major role in her life. I pray that sometimes she can let go the traumas of the past, and that horses will be an important part in her life, but not THE only defining element in her life.

Animals Healing Power

My-mindguide.com

INTRODUCTION

It is a little-known fact that animals frequently heal the wounds of loneliness and trauma in our society. Pets can be lifesavers, satisfying not just our needs for companionship and to feel loved but also our deep desire to love in return. Of course, this does not only apply to people who are alone. Even those blessed with many human companions hold a particular affinity for their pets.

Those who own pets are well aware that they make us happy. However, a growing body of scientific data indicates that our pets can help make us healthier. This helps explain why animals—primarily dogs and cats, birds, fish, and even horses—are increasingly used in settings ranging from hospitals and nursing homes to schools, jails, and mental institutions.

Experiencing a wide range of emotions is natural and appropriate, but pets can help curb negative thoughts. According to studies, simply looking into your pet's eyes can reduce your heart rate. Their mere presence is enough to calm you down, warm you up, and make you feel cherished with unconditional love. One beautiful example is companion dogs trained to sense impending panic attacks and assist veterans with other anxiety issues. Equine-assisted therapy (horse-assisted therapy) is also making great strides toward helping troubled teens and suffering adults. Companion animals assist people with special needs by giving care that humans cannot or will not provide. More and more people recognize the need for "emotional support animals" that serve various functions. It is undeniable that most people find comfort in close contact with friendly animals.

According to research, people who engage with animals may have higher levels of oxytocin (also known as the "trust hormone," "love hormone," or "bonding hormone"). In an example, one study discovered that simply making eye contact with their dogs when they returned home from work enhanced oxytocin levels in a group of women. On an emotional level, oxytocin assists mothers in bonding with their newborn offspring, aids human couples in developing a more profound sense of intimacy, and has been connected to improved feelings of self-esteem, optimism, and trust.

In addition to oxytocin, there is some evidence that forming a connection with a friendly animal can lower cortisol, the stress hormone, and increase levels of dopamine, the feel-good brain chemical. Given these advantages, it's no surprise that animals are now being used in various therapeutic procedures and programs. You've probably heard of programs that bring animals directly into hospitals to help cheer up, relax, and entertain patients.

Interestingly, even though animals can improve mental and physical health, we continue to use phrases like "stop acting like an animal," as if animals were somehow beneath us. Such terminology is scientifically incorrect.

No other animal degrades its surroundings in the same way that people do. In fact, in their natural state, each animal species contributes to the broader ecosystem, aiding in preserving the planet's equilibrium. Only when a foreign species is introduced and becomes invasive, causing an ecological imbalance, do you see a species damaging the environment. So, the true question is: Do we continue to participate in the annihilation of humanity—our own species—and others with whom we share our planet? Or do we begin to act like other animals to achieve balance?

Animals are frequently regarded as hazardous. However, when it comes to the deadliest animals on the earth, those most feared for taking human lives—such as sharks, wolves, and bears—are nowhere near the top of the list. However, human beings are at the absolute pinnacle, ahead of even disease-carrying mosquitos.

THE HEALING POWER
OF ANIMALS

The concept that animals have unique healing abilities is nothing new to us. For many years, their restorative force has been written about, filmed, and documented in various other ways. According to NPR, the use of pets in medicine extends back more than 150 years, as per Aubrey Fine, a clinical psychologist, and professor at California State Polytechnic

University. Studies dating back three decades confirm that the simple act of petting one's dog can lower blood pressure. More recently, studies have focused on the relationship between interacting with animals and the release of the hormone oxytocin, which has powerful effects on the body's abilities to heal and grow new cells.

However, this is not where the benefits of having a pet end in terms of healing. Often, those who have pets are more likely to include additional exercise in their routines, something I am well aware of since spending a significant amount of time running through my home and up and down the street with my pets! However, aside from the physical benefits, owning a pet also helps humans realize that love can be unconditional! Animals do not pass judgment or criticize you based on your appearance, the way you dress, your political opinions, or world views. No such things exist in the animal realm; therefore, it is unimportant.

The only thing animals appear to want from their owners (apart from life-sustaining requirements like a fresh supply of food and water) is to spend time with them and love them for who they are—unconditionally. Consider this: What a wonderful life lesson it would be if all of us could act as our pets do—without even trying. To simply BE! To exist unapologetically and fully. There would be no judgment, only love and acceptance. Through this perspective, the immensity of the possibility settles in. Humans should strive to be more like animals by existing in the present moment and living based on unconditional love and acceptance.

Rabbit

My-mindguide.com

WHAT DOES THE RESEARCH SAY?

The research clearly indicates that having an animal in your life is beneficial to your physical health. There is no denying that. It is well established that having an animal in our lives can result in fewer doctor visits, reduced blood pressure, lower cholesterol levels, and a lower risk of dying from a heart attack. Animals in our homes and hearts make us healthier!

Animals are beneficial for child development.
Many parents believe that adding a four-legged pet to the family is beneficial to the children. They are, for the most part, correct. Children who interact with animals regularly develop stronger self-esteem, participate in more activities such as sports, hobbies, clubs, or housework, and develop more loving behavior. They are also more compassionate toward both animals and humans.

Now, I'm certainly not advocating that everyone rush out and get little Johnny a horse without first considering the cost and time constraints involved. Pets don't work for every family in every living situation, and some pets will work for some but not others. Choosing a pet requires a great deal of planning and preparation, careful selection, and consideration of your own unique family and housing circumstances. However, if you can find the right pet for your home, adding an animal to your family can provide your children with valuable opportunities to learn about life, responsibility, and nurturing and caring for others.

Animals are good for seniors.
Seniors who own pets are less likely to need to see the doctor frequently, manage their stress better, are more active, and are significantly less lonely.

Animals can be good for our marriages.
According to one study, couples who have a dog at home have developed a stronger bond with each other as well.

While most research indicates the benefits are most prominent when there is a positive interaction between the person and the animal, some studies show that being in the presence of an animal, even ones we don't know or engage with directly, can have a favorable impact. Children were instructed to read aloud in front of an audience in one study. The mere presence of a friendly dog dramatically decreased the children's stress levels.

The company of an animal can also cause us to treat one other more kindly, generously, compassionately, and see each other in a more positive light. For example, people in wheelchairs or with disabilities who have a dog accompanying them experience considerably more positive social contacts and interactions than those unaccompanied. Others are more likely to approach and socialize with them rather than ignore or shun them.

Animals can even make us smarter.
Animals have been studied to see how they can aid in language acquisition and verbal abilities in early childhood, as well as stimulate and drive cognitive development.

Animals help us most during times of challenge.
Animals can improve our physical and emotional health at any time. Still, the following quote from the book *Animals as Teachers and Healers* by Susan Chernak McElroy expresses that this bond is especially powerful when we are feeling vulnerable, stressed, or facing a challenge, loss, or significant change in our lives:

"I was treated for depression in my early twenties, following a suicide attempt. I had shock treatment and intensive medication for two years and never left the house except to see the therapist. During those years, Sunshine was my lone buddy and the only living entity who could communicate with me. I caressed her, hummed to her, murmured to her, and cried into her fur. When it looked like the entire world was sleeping without me, she'd keep an eye on me. She was the only completely secure entity in my universe. I'm now in my forties. Years of good health and faith have given me what I couldn't have imagined when I was twenty. Sunshine has been gone for a long time. Maybe she didn't heal me, but she did save me so that I could heal myself with time and strength."

Again, evidence verifies the remarkable healing potential of an animal's love and support, which Sunshine's human companion has expressed. Here are a few additional examples:

- AIDS patients who have pets experience less despair and stress. Their dogs are a massive source of comfort for them and help them believe in their coping abilities.

- Children with autism who have dogs exhibit "more pro-social behaviors and less autistic traits such as self-absorption."

- Other research has found that animals can act as a buffer variable for a child's stressful experience, such as war or sexual abuse.

- Several studies have shown that companion animals serve as a buffer against depression, reduce the likelihood of maladaptive behaviors and suicide, motivate individuals to engage in more healthy and constructive activities, and assist us in gaining insight into our emotional experiences, illness, and behavior.

- Finally, having an animal as a companion can help children cope with the terrible illness or loss of a parent.

At times like these, we may seek the assistance of a counselor or another member of the helping professions. It is easy to understand how including animals in these professions could improve growth and healing.

Pet Partners (formerly the Delta Society), a non-profit organization dedicated to exploring and improving human-animal interactions, refers to the inclusion of animals in treatment programs as animal-assisted therapy (AAT). Animal-assisted therapy can be defined as "a goal-oriented intervention in which an animal is an integral part of the treatment process, which is designed to promote improvement in human physical, social, emotional, and/or cognitive functioning." Many practitioners and programs, ranging from therapeutic horseback riding to pet visitation programs in hospitals, are discovering that animals can often reach out to, connect with, and aid people in ways that humans are only beginning to comprehend.

WAYS PETS MAKE A DIFFERENCE IN YOUR LIFE

Life is priceless. We are constantly looking for ways to extend and improve our lives. Pets provide us with companionship and unconditional affection, but they also play an essential role in improving the quality of our lives.

Getting a pet is one of the best decisions you can make. There is nothing quite like being woken up by your dog standing before you with big black innocent eyes, looking at you with adoration, tongue hanging out sideways or holding a toy in its mouth, nose in your face, ears all pointy or floppy, and tail wagging at the speed of 100 repetitions per minute. The feeling of happiness can be felt and recalled but cannot be expressed in words.

Have you ever felt like the world has come crashing down on you, and you can't seem to stop the tears or relieve the agony in your chest no matter what you do? Have you had the blessing of a pet come and soothe you at that time? I used to get nervous before exams. I would sit at my desk until late at night studying and sometimes crying because it's just too much sometimes. There are too many expectations, unread chapters, unfulfilled dreams, pressure, and way too much disappointment. It's all just too much! When I felt the loneliest during those long nights, I was so fortunate that my loving pet dog came and sat there with me. He sat near my feet, his head brushing my toes, licking my feet, and attempting to comfort me, always ready for a hug. He'd roll over, bring his favorite toy and give it to me, or keep pushing my chair and playing around it. Ultimately, I'd give up and give in. I'd pretend that I fell from the chair, and then he'd come racing, all frightened, until the moment he realized I was tricking him, then he'd simply walk away. The drama, love, and fun are limitless when you have a pet.

According to a study published in the Journal of Personality and Social Psychology, pet owners had higher self-esteem than non-pet owners. Pet owners are also more extroverted and less fearful than non-pet owners. Another study on ninety-seven pet owners subjected participants to a poor social experience. Afterward, they were instructed to write about their best friend or create a map of their college campus. According to the findings of this study, those who wrote about their pet or closest friend had no negative thoughts and were equally joyful, even after the unfavorable social encounter. Studies have also shown that pet owners with cardiac problems are less likely to have a heart attack than others. Further, the use of therapy dogs to treat anxiety and chronic pain has seen remarkable benefits.

When you have a pet, you always have someone to cuddle with, someone to listen without complaining as you vent out your frustrations, someone to distract you from life's worries, someone to go on a walk with, and someone always waiting at home for your arrival. Most importantly, you always have someone to love you unconditionally. Being around an animal not only lowers your blood pressure, which is one physical marker of stress, but it also helps enhance serotonin and dopamine levels in your brain. These molecules are associated with feelings of happiness, tenderness, and contentment. Pets appear to boost the emotions that make you more capable of dealing with adverse life situations. Other advantages to having a pet include developing a higher sense of responsibility and more effective time management skills.

You don't have to go out and purchase the most costly breed of dog or cat to find a good fit! This fixation with exotic breeds that make a status statement isn't what owning a pet is all about. The Indian stray, also known as the native Indie dog, is a versatile breed that is also one of the healthiest. They stand in stark contrast to St. Bernards and Huskies, which are not suited to warmer climates, or Labradors and German Sheppards, which resulted from uncontrolled and exploitative inbreeding and, as such, are prone to a variety of genetic medical issues. Every year, 2.7 million dogs are euthanized in shelters due to a lack of people willing to adopt them. When you adopt from a shelter or rescue group, you save that dog and make room for another animal in need. Adopt a dog from a shelter or the streets near you; they all deserve love and a safe home. A stray's life on the streets is riddled with abuse and starvation, generally cut short by a human hand. Giving such a dog a home is like giving them the gift of life.

Here are ways our pets improve our life regularly:

1. **Health Benefits** – When you're at home, it's nearly impossible to ignore your pet, who is almost certainly pleading for your attention. Even after a long day at work, it's difficult to lie on

the couch or in bed without giving your pet at least *some* attention. Most pets are pretty persistent! When you have a lively dog, you are more likely to go on daily walks and be more active. If you have a furry companion, you will inevitably drag a toy across the room for enjoyment. This frequent activity has been shown to lower blood pressure and make you less likely to develop heart disease.

2. **Stress Reduction** – Petting your dog or cat causes the increased production of a relaxation hormone, which helps to soothe and relieve tension while also potentially decreasing your blood pressure. Studies have shown that pets can relieve stress more effectively than even human help in certain situations. People may seek extra assistance from their dog companions, which makes a good deal of sense… After all, isn't it guaranteed that your pet will not judge you?

3. **Companionship** – It's a beautiful feeling to know that no matter how you feel or look on any given day, someone is always there for you unconditionally. And if you have a pet, you know what I'm talking about. Pets provide a sense of belonging and importance in your life, making you feel less alone in the world. Pets are an excellent shield against loneliness.

4. **Social Fulfillment** – Face the facts. Pets are constantly the center of our attention, and whether you're entertained just by watching them or talking about them, whether they're present or not, they will always help you connect with people.

5. **Happiness** – The unconditional affection and respect shown by a pet make us feel supported and enable us to be happier, less negative people.

6. **Lower Risk of Allergies** – Surprisingly, studies have found that being exposed to pets as a child reduces the likelihood of acquiring allergies. A study conducted by the University of Wisconsin's Department of Pediatrics discovered that early exposure to dogs reduced the risk of developing several allergic illnesses.

Cat

THE BENEFITS OF PETS

Most pet owners know the numerous benefits of sharing their lives with companion animals. However, many are ignorant of the physical and emotional health benefits that accompany snuggling up to a furry buddy. Only recently have studies begun to scientifically investigate the benefits of this type of human-animal interaction.

Pets have evolved to be intensely sensitive to humans, including our behavior and emotions. Dogs, for example, can understand many of the words we speak, but they excel at deciphering our tone of voice, body language, and gestures. A devoted dog, like any good human companion, will glance into your eyes to assess your emotional condition and attempt to understand what you're thinking and feeling (and to work out when the next walk or treat might be coming, of course).

Pets, particularly dogs and cats, can reduce stress, anxiety, and depression, alleviate loneliness, promote better exercise habits, add more fun, and even improve cardiovascular health. Caring for an animal can help children become more secure and active as they grow up. Pets can also provide essential company for elderly people who often face loneliness. Perhaps most importantly, a pet can bring you genuine delight and unconditional love.

Any pet can improve your health. While it's true that people with pets often experience more significant health benefits than those without, a pet doesn't necessarily have to be a dog or a cat. A rabbit could be ideal if you're allergic to other animals or have limited space but still want a furry friend to snuggle with. Birds can encourage social interaction and help keep your mind sharp if you're an older adult. Snakes, lizards, and other reptiles can make for exotic companions. Even watching fish in an aquarium can help reduce muscle tension and lower your pulse rate.

Studies have shown that:

- Pet owners are less likely to be depressed than non-pet owners.

- People who have pets have lower blood pressure in stressful conditions than those who do not have pets. One study discovered that when people diagnosed with borderline hypertension adopted dogs from a shelter, their blood pressure dropped considerably after five months.

- Playing with a dog, cat, or other pet can increase serotonin and dopamine levels, which soothe and relax.

- Triglyceride and cholesterol levels (indicators of heart disease) are lower in pet owners than in non-pet owners.

- Patients who have experienced heart attacks and have pets live longer than those who do not.

- Pet owners over the age of 65 visit their doctors 30% less frequently than those who do not own a pet.

One of the reasons for these therapeutic effects is that companion animals satisfy a fundamental human desire for touch. Even hardened offenders in prison can exhibit long-term behavioral changes after interacting with dogs, with many of them experiencing mutual affection for the first time. When you're tense or anxious, caressing, hugging, or otherwise touching a loved animal can quickly relax and comfort you. Pet companionship can help alleviate loneliness, and most dogs are excellent stimuli for incorporating more healthy activity into your life, which can significantly improve mood and alleviate sadness.

Increase Self-Esteem

According to studies, children who have family pets have stronger levels of self-esteem. Why? Probably because they have a four-legged (or two-legged) critter to love and a pal to chat and play with when no one else is around.

Pets can also promote self-esteem by alleviating social isolation. Rejection hurts, but it goes away when you're met with a wagging tail. And studies demonstrate that pets contribute to our sense of belonging. According to one study, pet owners have higher self-esteem, are more conscientious, and recover faster from social rejection. It's no surprise dogs are regarded as men's (and women's) best friends.

Boost the Immune System

Believe it or not, petting a dog may even be enough to keep that annoying cold at bay. Those who were asked to pet dogs reported an improvement in their overall health, particularly their immune systems (as opposed to those asked pet stuffed animals or nothing at all).

Decrease Anxiety, Pain, and Depression

Pet therapy, also known as animal-assisted therapy (AAT), has been associated with reduced anxiety, pain, and sadness in patients suffering from various mental or physical health issues. Patients enduring chemotherapy, veterans suffering from post-traumatic stress disorder, and physical therapy patients working on fine motor skills benefit from pet therapy. Some academic institutions are taking notice as well. Students at Miami University can participate in pet therapy sessions to help them cope with homesickness and despair. During midterms and finals, when stress levels are at an all-time high, dogs are "on-call" to help students manage their feelings of worry and anxiety.

Decrease Stress and Conquer Addiction

Yes, we all know that our pets can make us happy, but studies suggest associating with dogs can help lower stress. Even simple activities like playing fetch or petting your dog can reduce the production of cortisol, a stress hormone, and boost the quantity of the feel-good hormone oxytocin in your brain as it is linked to emotional bonding.

Petting an animal can help humans and animals relax and reduce stress levels. Because of the release of oxytocin, it is believed that an animal's heart rate lowers, and blood pressure drops along with a person's.

Stress and addiction have comparable effects on the brain, so dealing with one usually involves tackling the other. Life's pressures might cause cravings or a relapse, so it's critical to remain calm, especially if there is a history of addiction. Getting close to a pet is an excellent approach to relieve stress and help combat the urge to return to substance abuse.

Decrease Blood Pressure

High blood pressure is commonly misunderstood as a problem that only the elderly face, but in reality, everyone can benefit from keeping their levels in check. "The simple act of caressing an animal is known to induce a person's blood pressure to drop," says Alan Beck, director of Purdue University's Center for the Human-Animal Bond. We like to think that means we're one step closer to acquiring a prescription for dog cuddles.

According to the American Heart Association, there is a link between contact with a pet (especially dogs) and a reduced risk for heart disease and greater longevity. The National Institute of Health's review of heart-related studies on people who have pets showed that pet owners had decreased levels of cholesterol, triglycerides, and blood pressure—all of which may minimize the risk of a heart attack in the future.

Improved Social Interaction

Pets can assist you in your social life! It is especially true for dog owners because their dogs get them out and about on walks and at the park. When you have a dog with you, people appear to be more inclined to communicate, and the topic of dogs is a good icebreaker in terms of conversation. Animals are a terrific way to connect with others in social circumstances, and they may even aid those who struggle with social shyness

PETS CAN HELP YOU MAKE HEALTHY LIFESTYLE CHANGES

Adopting healthy lifestyle modifications can help alleviate depression, anxiety, stress, bipolar disorder, and PTSD symptoms. Caring for a pet can assist you in adopting a healthier lifestyle by:

Increasing Exercise

Taking your dog for a walk, hike, or run is a fun and satisfying way to fit in daily exercise. According to studies, dog owners are considerably more likely to meet their daily activity requirements—and exercising every day is also beneficial to the animal. It will strengthen your bond, eliminate most dog behavioral issues, and keep your companion fit and healthy.

Providing Companionship

Having adequate companionship can help you avoid sickness and possibly add years to your life, whereas loneliness and isolation can provoke depression symptoms and contribute to growing health issues. Caring for an animal can help you feel desired and loved while diverting your attention away from your troubles, especially if you live alone. Most dog and cat owners communicate with their pets, and some even utilize them to work through problems. Coming home to a wagging tail or purring cat beats loneliness every time.

Making Human Connections Through Pets

Pets may be an excellent social lubricant for their owners, assisting in forming and maintaining new friendships. On walks, treks, or at a dog park, dog owners commonly stop and talk to one another. Pet owners can also meet new individuals by going to pet stores, clubs, and training programs. They may even connect with others in online groups for people with a shared interest in pets and animals.

Reducing Anxiety

It doesn't hurt to reiterate just how much comfort, anxiety relief, and self-confidence can be provided through animal companionship, particularly for people afraid to venture out into the world. Pets can help you become more conscious and appreciate the delight of the present because they tend to live in the moment. Unlike most human beings, pets don't worry about what occurred yesterday or what might happen tomorrow.

Maintaining Structure and Routine

Most pets, particularly dogs, require a consistent feeding and exercise routine. A steady routine keeps an animal healthy and calm—and it may do the same for you. Whether you're unhappy, anxious, or upset, one plaintive glance from your pet will get you out of bed to feed, exercise, and care for them.

Providing Sensory Stress Relief

Touch and movement are two excellent methods to relieve stress rapidly. Stroking a dog, cat, or another animal can instantly drop your blood pressure and make you feel calmer and less agitated.

The Benefits of Pets for Older Adults

Aside from offering essential companionship, owning a pet can play a crucial role in healthy aging by assisting you to:

Find Meaning and Joy in Life

As you age, people often lose things that once occupied their time and gave life meaning. You could retire from your job, or your children could relocate far away. Caring for a pet can be enjoyable and beneficial to your morale, optimism, and sense of self-worth. Choosing to adopt a pet from a shelter, especially an older pet, might increase your feelings of accomplishment. You've adopted a pet that would otherwise have been euthanized or spent the remainder of its life in the shelter system.

Stay Connected

Maintaining a social network as you get older isn't always easy. Retirement, illness, death, and relocation can all result in the loss of close friends and family members. It can also be challenging to make new friends. Pets, particularly dogs, are an excellent way for older folks to strike up conversations and meet new people.

Boost Vitality

You may overcome many physical obstacles connected with aging by taking care of yourself. Dogs, cats, and other pets promote playfulness, laughter, and exercise, all of which can help enhance your immune system and raise your energy.

The Benefits of Pets for Children

Children who grow up with dogs not only have a lower chance of allergies and asthma, but they also learn responsibility, compassion, and empathy.

- Unlike parents or teachers, Pets are never critical and do not give directives. They are always affectionate, and their sheer presence at home can help children feel secure. When mom and dad aren't there, having a constant companion might help children cope with separation anxiety.

- A pet's love and company can make a child feel valued and aid in developing a healthy self-image.

- Children who have an emotional attachment to their pets are better equipped to form relationships with others.

- Pets have been demonstrated in studies to help calm hyperactive or angry children. Of course, both the animal and the child must be trained to interact responsibly.

Children, like adults, can benefit from the simple act of playing with a pet. It can provide calmness and relaxation and stimulate the brain and body. Playing with a pet might even be a gateway to learning for a child. It can pique a child's imagination and curiosity. The rewards of teaching a dog a new skill, for example, can teach children the value of perseverance. Caring for a furry pet can also provide a child with a lot of joy and a sense of personal responsibility.

Children with Learning Disorders and Other Challenges

Children with autism or learning disabilities may interact better with dogs than with people. Autistic children, like animals, frequently rely on nonverbal signs to communicate. Learning to bond with a pet first may even help an autistic child interact with others.

Pets can assist children with learning difficulties to better manage stress and relax themselves, preparing them to face the challenges of their disorder. Furthermore, playing and exercising with a pet can assist children who have trouble focusing with remaining aware and attentive throughout the day. It can also be an excellent antidote to the stress and frustration brought on by a learning disability.

Owning a Pet is a Major Commitment

Despite all of the advantages to pet ownership, it is crucial to remember that a pet is not a cure-all for mental health difficulties. Owning a pet is valuable and reassuring only for people who love and appreciate domestic animals and have the time and resources to maintain a pet. Keeping your pet happy and healthy is essential. If you're not an "animal person," owning a pet will not give you any health benefits or improve your life. It will likely have the opposite effect.

Even if you adore animals, before taking the plunge and getting a pet, you must have a firm grasp of everything that comes with caring for a pet. Owning a pet is a significant commitment that will endure through the animal's lifetime, which may be ten or fifteen years in the case of dogs, possibly longer for other pets. At the end of that commitment, you'll have to deal with the pain and mourning that comes with losing a loved one. Grief over the loss of a pet can be devastating.

Other drawbacks to owning a pet include:

Additional Expenses

The costs associated with pet food, veterinary care, licenses, grooming costs, toys, bedding, boarding fees, and other maintenance expenses can mount up quickly. If you're unemployed, elderly, or on a limited fixed income, it may be a struggle to cope with the expense of pet ownership.

Extra Time and Attention

Coming home to a dog who has been cooped up in the house alone all day is hardly therapeutic, as any dog owner will tell you. Dogs require daily exercise to keep calm and balanced. Most other pets require daily care and attention, some more than others.

Reduction in Social Activities

A dog can only be left alone for a certain amount of time. You'll be allowed to take your dog with you to visit friends, run errands, or wait outside a coffee shop if you train him properly, but you won't be able to go away for a weekend without previously arranging care for your pet. It makes it more difficult to be spontaneous.

Destructive Tendencies

Any pet can—and probably will—have an accident at home on occasion. Some cats are prone to tearing upholstery, while others are prone to chew shoes. While training can help eliminate negative, destructive behavior, it is widespread in animals left alone for extended periods with little exercise or stimulation.

Greater Responsibility

Most dogs, regardless of size or breed, are capable of causing injury to people if their owners do not handle them correctly. Cats, too, can scratch or bite. Pet owners must be on the lookout for potential hazards, especially in the presence of children.

Certain Health Risks

While some diseases can be transmitted from cats and dogs to their human owners, allergies are the most common health risk associated with pet ownership. Before committing to pet ownership, if you or a family member has been diagnosed with a pet allergy, carefully evaluate whether you can live with the symptoms. Also, consider that if you have a pet, certain friends or relatives who have allergies may be unable to visit you. Many pets are returned because their owners realized they could not handle their allergies or those of their family and friends.

Mouse

ANIMALS HELPING PEOPLE

Animals provide a sense of security and comfort. Therapy dogs, in particular, excel at this aspect of helping human beings. Because of this, they are frequently taken into hospitals or nursing homes to assist people in coping with stress and anxiety.

"Dogs are everywhere," Dr. Ann Berger, a physician and researcher at the National Institute of Health Clinical Center in Bethesda, Maryland, says. "If someone is dealing with anything, they know how to be there and be kind. Their entire attention is focused on the person." Berger works with cancer patients and people at the end of their lives. She teaches them how to practice mindfulness to help them cope with stress and discomfort.

"Attention, intention, compassion, and awareness are the cornerstones of mindfulness," Berger explains. "Animals bring all of those things to the table. It's something that people have to get used to. This is something that animals do naturally."

While their comforting presence is undeniable, animals may expose people to more germs; therefore, researchers continue to assess the safety of bringing them inside hospitals. A recent study is looking into the safety of bringing dogs to visit children with cancer. As part of the study, scientists carefully examine the children's hands after a canine visit to discover if harmful levels of germs were passed from the dog.

Dogs may also be helpful in the classroom setting. According to one study, dogs can assist children with ADHD in focusing their attention more effectively. Two groups of youngsters with ADHD were enrolled in 12-week group treatment sessions by the researchers. The first set of children spent thirty minutes reading to a therapy dog each week. The second group read aloud to dog-shaped puppets. Children who read to real animals demonstrated improved social skills, sharing, cooperation, and volunteerism. They experienced fewer behavioral issues as well.

Another study indicated that children with autism spectrum disorder were calmer in the classroom while interacting with guinea pigs. After spending just ten minutes in supervised group playtime with guinea pigs, the children's anxiety levels decreased. In addition, the youngsters had improved social connections and were more engaged with their peers. According to the researchers, the animals provided unconditional acceptance, making them a soothing comfort to the children.

Animals can serve as a bridge between those social connections. Researchers are working to better understand these impacts and who they may benefit most and assist human beings in many unexpected ways. According to a recent study, caring for fish helped diabetic youth control their disease. Researchers had a group of type 1 diabetic kids feed and monitor the water levels of a pet fish twice a day. Every week, the tank water had to be changed as part of the caretaking routine. This was done in conjunction with the kids going through their blood glucose (blood sugar) diaries with their parents.

Researchers looked at how often these teenagers tested their blood glucose levels. The fish-keeping youth were more rigorous about checking their blood glucose levels, which is critical for preserving their health, than those who were not given a fish to care for.

While pets can provide various health benefits, they may not be suitable for everyone. Recent research suggests that early contact with pets may help prevent allergies and asthma in young children. However, having dogs in the house can cause more harm than benefit for people who are allergic to specific animals.

Helping Each Other

Pets come with a whole list of obligations. Having a pet requires you to care for and feed it. The National Institutes of Health/ Mars funds research into the consequences of human-animal interactions on both the pet and the person.

It's important to remember that animals can experience stress and exhaustion, just like humans. Children must learn to spot indications of worry in their pets and know when not to approach them. Animal bites can be quite dangerous, but they rarely occur without warning. Dog bite prevention is an issue that parents should think about, especially for young children who aren't always aware of what is and isn't proper to do with a dog. There are many resources available that can help educate children on interacting with animals safely. The library, the internet, and your local shelter or pet store are all likely to have materials available to help in this area.

Researchers will continue to look at the many health benefits owning a pet may provide.

THE HEALING POWER OF ANIMALS AND TEENS MENTAL HEALTH

Young people who form connections with animals can diminish their nervousness, melancholy, and dejection to achieve a better quality of life. For adolescents endeavoring to keep up with their emotional well-being, a basic association with animals or a pet can adjust the frame of mind of those with mental issues. In addition, connecting with an animal can help youngsters with mental issues become more engaged with their current circumstances in harmless ways.

For example, at Paradigm Treatment, Gator the treatment dog has "an unparalleled capacity to bring the spirit of the gathering up," said Robert Burns, an instructor at the Point Dume program. "On our hardest days, Gator blasts through the study hall entryway and finds the child who is struggling and in the most over-the-top critical need of help," Robert said. "His essence has been, perhaps, my most prominent apparatus in supporting the young during troublesome and emotional occasions."

Pets and animals can assist individuals in dealing with drawn-out psychological conditions, as per the Human-Animal Bond Research Institute (HABRI), a non-profit examination and instruction association that shares logical exploration to show the positive effects on wellbeing pets can generate. The accompanying data, provided by HABRI, offers more insights concerning the impact that animals can have on a young person's life:

The Role of Pets in Managing the Mental Health of Teenagers
Pet owner teens experienced an immediate sense of tranquility and therapeutic benefit from their pets' consistent presence and close physical proximity. The role of pets in the social networks of people managing a long-term mental health problem was investigated in a 2016 study. The study discovered that pets helped people adopt habits that provided emotional and social support over time.

- Pets provide the opportunity to develop a sense of control that comes with pet ownership.

- Pets provide a sense of stability and routine that evolves through time in the relationship, reinforcing stable cognitions from the assurance that people could turn to and rely on pets in times of need.

- Pets provide stability by giving individual experiences a feeling of order and continuity and creating a sense of meaning in one's life.

- For those who care for them, pets provide a distraction and disturbance from uncomfortable symptoms like hearing voices, suicidal thoughts, and contemplating self-harm while facilitating a sense of regularity and exercise.

Social Support

Given the evidence linking social isolation to poor mental health and the loss of friendships, researchers have looked at the effects of companion animals as social facilitators or catalysts for forming friendships or social support networks.

Pet owners were found to be a significant aspect in building healthy neighborhoods in a study on the role of pets as facilitators of getting to know people, friendship creation, and social support networks.

- Pet owners were substantially more likely than non-pet owners to know their neighbors.

- Around 40% of pet owners said people they met through their pet provided them with one or more sorts of social assistance (emotional, informational, or instrumental).

- Many pet owners found that their pets helped them build relationships that provided them with tangible types of social assistance, both practical and emotional.

Loneliness

Pet ownership has been linked to increased social contact and interaction and a stronger sense of community friendliness. Pet owners achieve higher scores on social capital and civic engagement scales, implying that having a pet creates an opportunity for neighbors to interact.

Stress

The impact of human-animal interaction has been demonstrated by reduced stress-related parameters such as epinephrine and norepinephrine, improved immune system functioning, better pain management, increased trustworthiness, more trust toward others, reduced aggression, enhanced empathy, and improved learning.

Many studies include a brief stressor, such as solving a complex math problem, to test the impact of pets on stress levels. One study looked at the effects of pet ownership on hypertension in people holding high-stress jobs and their cardiovascular reactions to psychological stress (mental arithmetic test). According to the findings of the study:

- The expanded living environment that pets often provide is likely to benefit people with limited social support systems.

- Pets offer non-evaluative social assistance that is essential for reducing stress-related psychological responses.

Another study looked at the bio-behavioral stress response, which included systolic and diastolic blood pressure, heart rate, salivary cortisol, SBP, DBP, HR, and self-reported anxiety and stress for therapy-dog owners interacting with their dog and therapy-dog owners interacting with a stranger. The findings support a buffering effect on the stress response associated with owners interacting with their dogs, which may also apply to encounters with unfamiliar therapy dogs:

- During the intervention, the therapy-dog owners reported less anxiety and worry.

- Physiological measures were lower in the group that had never met a therapy dog before.

- Positive feelings for dogs were linked to lower levels of self-reported stress, salivary cortisol (a biological stress marker), and SBP.

Anxiety

Many studies on the effects of pets and human-animal interaction on anxiety focus on hospital patients, who are typically more prone to anxiety.

- Patients who were provided with a therapy dog visit for twelve minutes had significantly lower systolic pulmonary artery pressure during and after the intervention, as well as pulmonary capillary wedge pressure during and after the intervention, according to a study of hospitalized heart failure patients.

- Compared to the control groups, patients who had a therapy dog visit experienced the highest drop in state anxiety sum score from the baseline.

PETS AND MENTAL HEALTH

Human-animal relationships are powerful. And there's no denying that pets and mental health go hand-in-hand. According to a Harris poll from 2015, 95% of pet owners consider their animal to be a family member. That is true regardless of our age. Pets bring joy to children, teenagers, adults, and elders alike. As a result, pets and mental health are inextricably linked.

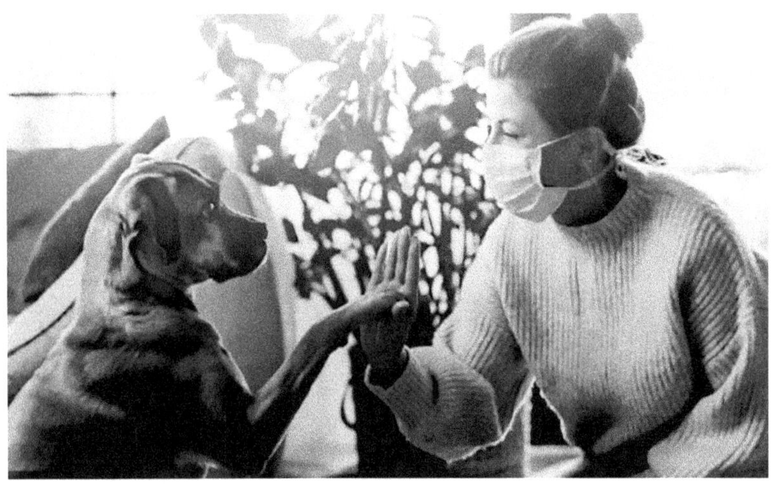

Furthermore, scientific research has demonstrated the mental health benefits of keeping a dog or cat. Animals can aid in the treatment of depression, anxiety, and stress. They also provide companionship and help to alleviate loneliness. Pets also provide us with delight and unconditional love.

Early Research on Pets and Mental Health

Thirty years ago, the first study on pets and mental health was published. The research was carried out by Purdue University psychologist Alan Beck and University of Pennsylvania psychiatrist Aaron Katcher. This research examined what occurs to a person's body when they pet a friendly dog. What they discovered was:

- Blood pressure went down
- Heart rate slowed
- Breathing became more regular
- Muscle tension relaxed

All of these result from a lower stress level; therefore, the researchers revealed concrete proof of several extraordinary mental health benefits of keeping pets.

The Power of Animal-Assisted Therapy

Since those early studies, researchers have learned more about the link between pets and human mental health. As a result, animal-assisted therapy programs have emerged as a vital component of mental health care. Individuals who own mental health animals, such as an emotional support dog, also benefit.

Equine therapy has been used in teen mental health programs since the 1990s. Equine-Assisted Therapy uses horses to help people with mental illnesses cope and improve their symptoms. The human-horse bond allows teenagers to talk about their feelings and problems. They accomplish this through a profound, direct nonverbal communication experience.

However, we can also benefit from pet therapy every day in the comfort of our own homes. Pets are not only great companions, but they are also beneficial to your physical and mental health. Of course, if you are having trouble taking care of yourself, you should consult your doctor before getting a pet.

Let's take a more detailed look at how pets support our mental health.

Interacting with Pets Lowers Our Stress Hormones
According to studies on pets and mental health, petting and playing with animals reduces stress-related chemicals. These advantages can be realized after only five minutes of interaction with a pet. As a result, pets are incredibly beneficial to anxiety sufferers.

Our serotonin and dopamine levels rise when we play with a dog or cat. These are hormones that help the nervous system relax and quiet down. We can help trigger the release of these "happy hormones" by smiling and laughing at our pets' charming behavior and comical antics.

Interacting with a friendly dog also lowers cortisol levels, a stress hormone. It also promotes the release of oxytocin, a hormone in the body that naturally relieves stress. It's for this reason that animal-assisted therapy is so effective.

Furthermore, caressing a pet decreases blood pressure because it is a sensory experience. As a result, it lowers stress levels. Research has shown that dogs can assist hyperactive or aggressive children to calm down.

In one study, a group of stressed-out adults was instructed to pet a rabbit, a turtle, or a toy. The toy did trigger any notable reaction when touched—stroking the rabbit or turtle, on the other hand, reduced stress. Furthermore, even those not very fond of animals reaped the benefits.

Pets Protect Against Childhood Anxiety

A pet dog might shield youngsters from feelings of anxiety, as per a study by the Centers for Disease Control and Prevention.

An aggregate of 643 children took part in the study. A significant portion of them had pet dogs in the home. Scientists estimated the youngsters' body mass index (BMI), anxiety levels, screen time, and activity. Subsequently, they observed that every one of the kids had comparable BMIs, screen time, and activity levels. This remained constant whether or not they had pet dogs. Yet, their anxiety levels were unique. Indeed, 21% of the kids who didn't have a pet dog tested positive on a text that evaluated anxiety levels., while just 12% of youngsters with dogs tested positive for anxiety.

The research is clear. Pets beneficially affect youth stress and nervousness. Accordingly, youngsters who grow up with pets might have a superior shot at becoming more cheerful and stable teenagers.

Our Pets Make Us Feel Needed

Individuals feel more needed when they have the responsibility of caring for a pet to focus on. The act of caretaking has shown many benefits to emotional wellbeing and a sense of responsibility that makes us feel valued. Focusing on another living thing provides us with a stronger sense of direction.

Moreover, this is valid in unique cases, even when the pet does not have a strong connection with its caregiver. For example, in a recent report around pets and emotional wellness, elderly individuals were given five crickets in an enclosure. Specialists observed their state of mind for approximately two months. Additionally, they contrasted them with a benchmark group that was not provided with any animals.

As a result of the study, the participants given crickets turned out to be less discouraged after two months than those in the benchmark group. Scientists presumed that the results indicated that focusing on a living animal created psychological wellness benefits—even without a deep connection between the human and animal. With this research in mind, it can be ascertained that doing things to benefit others—even crickets— lessens human feelings of misery and dejection.

Pets Increase Our Sense of Self-Esteem and Well-Being
Psychologists recently performed three studies on the benefits of pet ownership at Miami University and Saint Louis University. The results were published by the American Psychological Association.

Pet owners were found to have enhanced well-being in a variety of categories, according to the studies:

- Improved self-esteem
- Better physical fitness
- Fewer feelings of loneliness
- More conscientious and less preoccupied
- More extroverted
- Less fearful

In the principal study, 217 individuals addressed inquiries concerning their prosperity, character type, and connection style. Also, pet people were more joyful, content, and responded better to change than those who were not pet owners.

The subsequent study assessed 56 dog owners. Analysts investigated animal people's sentiments about their pets. Furthermore, they estimated their prosperity. One gathering of individuals announced that their dogs expanded their sensations of fitting in and having a "place," in addition to increasing their levels of confidence. Consequently, these members showed higher levels of general prosperity than those without pets.

In the subsequent study, 97 students with a mean age of 19 took part. Subsequently, scientists observed that pets could assist teenagers with feeling better in the wake of a breakup or other rejection.

The adolescents received some information about times when they felt avoided or rejected. Then, they were approached to do one of three things in writing: describe their beloved pet, discuss their most cherished human companion, or draw a map of their campus. It was determined that describing pets was similarly as powerful as writing about a trusted companion in fighting sensations of dismissal or rejection.

Cats and Dogs Are Great Examples of Living in the Moment
Pets live in the moment at all times. They don't stress over what happened yesterday. Additionally, they aren't worried about what may happen tomorrow. Thus, pets can assist individuals with being more mindful. They can guide people in living in the moment, rather than the past or future.

Pets can also assist with diverting teenagers' focus away from those things that are bothering them. They, essentially, act as a pleasant distraction from challenging situations. Further, investing energy in spending time with a pet assists teenagers with recalling how to be lively and lighthearted—something that can be forgotten amid adolescence.

Pets Support Recovery from Mental Illness

Pets benefit individuals recuperating from extreme issues connected to their emotional well-being. A new meta-examination examined seventeen scholastic papers drawn from nine clinical information bases. In doing so, specialists observed proof that having a pet provides significant advantages to individuals facing challenges to psychological well-being.

The papers determined that cats, dogs, hamsters, finches, and even goldfish impacted the psychological health of individuals living with dysfunctional behavior. Generally, the audit observed that pets assisted the participants with dealing with their feelings. Also, it diverted them from the potential side effects of their psychological well-being conditions.

For instance, a recent study at the University of Manchester in the United Kingdom included 54 participants diagnosed with severe psychological instabilities, like depression, schizophrenia, bipolar confusion, or post-traumatic stress disorder. Sixty percent of participants included a pet among their circle of most significant and strong connections. Additionally, a large portion of them said that pets assisted them with dealing with their ailment and regular day-to-day existence. Having pets provided them with a solid feeling of self-esteem and even districted them from symptoms such as hearing voices, self-destructive thoughts, or self-harming tendencies.

Focusing on a pet also gave owners a sense of responsibility and control. It provided them with the feeling that all was in order and scheduled, decreasing anxiety. One participant said, "When I was so discouraged, I was somewhat self-destructive. What made me stop was considering what the bunnies would do. That was the principal thing I considered… I can't leave this planet because the bunnies need me."

"Pets give a one-of-a-kind type of approval through unrestricted help, which they were frequently not getting from other family or social connections," said Dr. Helen Brooks, lead researcher of the review. Dr. Creeks and her group learned that pet ownership is helpful to achieving emotional wellness. In this manner, it ought to be consolidated into patient treatment plants whenever possible and appropriate.

Pets Help Us Build Healthy Habits

Pets must be cared for every day. Therefore, they assist us with building solid routines, schedules, and healthy habits.

Activity: Dog owners must regularly take their pets for walks, runs, and climbs. In this way, owners also get the advantages of exercise. Additionally, focusing on training every day is important to a dog's mental and physical wellbeing and can provide many benefits to the pet owner.

Time in Nature: Walking a dog or riding a horse gets us outside. Therefore, we experience the numerous emotional wellness advantages of connecting with animals and enjoying the outdoors, which can dramatically improve mental health.

Early Rising: Dogs and cats are happiest and healthiest when their needs are met following a standard timetable. Therefore, people who own pets must get up and meet these needs—regardless of their state of mind. Thus, pets motivate individuals to get up and begin their day at a reasonable hour.

Taking Care of Oneself: Caring for a dog, horse, cat, or another pet reminds us to focus on ourselves and our needs also. For instance, teenagers that hope to have their horses participate in Equine-Assisted Therapy must appreciate the significance of focusing on their wellbeing in addition to their pet's.

Our Pets Help Build Relationship Skills

Research shows that youngsters closely connected to their dogs form early memories about building associations with others. This can help with relationship-building later in life. Additionally, because dogs are quick to notice and comprehend human signals, they support children's enthusiasm. Dogs are very sensitive to their owners' mindsets and feelings.

Animals make socializing much easier for young children who find it challenging or unpleasant. One study analyzed the behavior of youngsters with a chemical imbalance in a study hall with a pet guinea pig. Specialists observed that these children were more friendly with their companions than similar children without homeroom pets. The children with the pet in the classroom also smiled and laughed significantly more frequently and showed fewer indications of being under stress.

Equine-Assisted Therapy also plays a crucial role in assisting adolescents with building relationship abilities. Teenagers make significant and powerful connections with their horses through horse-assisted therapy. The abilities they learn while connecting with their horses can enable them to connect more fully with loved ones. This is a fundamental stage in development and recovery.

Pets Support Social Connection

Another link between pets and emotional wellness, for both adults and youth, is that pets support social interaction and forming social connections. They alleviate social anxiety since they provide a commonly discussed topic that pet owners will feel comfortable talking about. Because of this, pets can neutralize social confinement and enable people to interact more easily with others, which can help them feel less lonely and isolated.

For instance, the simple act of walking a dog frequently prompts discussions with other dog owners during the process. Therefore, dog owners are generally more socially connected and less disengaged, improving their emotional well-being. Individuals who have more social connections and friendships will generally feel better overall and maintain an improved state of mind. There have been studies that indicate they may even be more advanced intellectually due to enhanced cognitive function.

The advantages of social connections include:
- Higher self-esteem
- Lower rates of anxiety and depression
- Happier, more optimistic outlook
- Stronger emotional regulation skills
- Improved cognitive function

- More empathy and feelings of trust toward others

Last But Not Least… Pets Give Us Unconditional Love

Dogs and cats love their owners unconditionally. For instance, pets don't have the slightest concern over how a teenager performed on a test. In addition, they don't pass judgment on adolescents' social abilities or athletic capacity. They are always glad to see their owners, regardless of what may happen in their lives. This unlimited and unconditional love is excellent for psychological well-being. It animates the cerebrum to deliver dopamine, the substance associated with feelings of joy.

In summary, the research and exploration into the links between pets and psychological wellness are clear. Consequently, individuals struggling with mental challenges should consider asking a specialist if a daily reassurance animal could be right for them.

Youths and adolescents that enjoy being affectionate with animals may enjoy working or volunteering at an animal shelter or a riding stable. This is particularly useful if it is impossible to have a pet in the home for one of several reasons.

REAL-LIFE STORIES OF THE HEALING POWER OF ANIMALS

To see how animals have the power to change our lives for the better, I have compiled a series of vignettes. Each of these stories reveals the powerful, life-changing connection that can be forged between man and animals of various species.

HEALING THROUGH HORSES

Christine and Her Horses

This story relates to me personally because it is about my sister, Christine, who is married, living in Italy with two lovely children, and is addicted to horses. And, yes, she has turned her whole family into horse enthusiasts as well.

She plays POLO CROSS at the professional level in Italy and owns six or seven horses. It is certainly not easy or cheap, and they struggle to pay for this hobby. While her husband is the primary "breadwinner," they both work to feed the horses—in addition to their family.

My sister was born in a state of chaos. My mom was pregnant when she got divorced. Yes, it was her ex-husband's child, but he refused to see her even once during his entire lifetime. What more could you possibly do to harm a young life?

During the first months of my sister's life, my mom started working to support our family, and I began taking care of Christine after school. I was only thirteen. I had to clean, bathe, and cook for all my siblings. The situation was far from ideal for a kid who knew his friends and schoolwork were waiting.

When she was one year old, she moved in with our grandparents because my mom was declared unfit to have young children in her custody due to medical/psychological issues. In addition, my mom remarried, started a career, and began living with her new husband, who was not eager to marry the whole package of a woman with four kids.

So, Christine grew up with her aging grandparents until she reached the age of seven, at which time she was placed in a Catholic boarding school managed by nuns. Nobody, including myself, had very much contact with her during those years. Her siblings saw little of her, and only on occasional weekends did her mother come and take her out. When my sister was approximately ten years old, my mom managed to show enough of a significant mental recovery that the court permitted her to begin taking care of her youngest daughter.

So, at around the age of ten, she moved in with her mom. Unfortunately, in doing so, she began living with her stepfather, who was attracted to her—and not in an appropriate fatherly way. Things continued this way for several years.

When she was eighteen, she finished school and contacted her older brother—me. We connected. However, I was also struggling to overcome various obstacles and had no real passion or love to offer this suffering, lonely little sister who was so full of hopes and dreams. I barely knew her.

She lived a couple of months in my apartment in Munich and worked in my advertising agency until she moved in with her Italian boyfriend. She was disappointed by my strange behavior and inability to show love or significant concern.

Once in Milano, Christine started a career and married her boyfriend. In Italy, however, you don't merely marry a groom. You marry the whole family. So, the marriage went sour after some family issues and ended after three years of unhappiness. Fortunately, no children were involved.

To distance herself from her youth and the pain of the past, Christine refused to speak German, her mother tongue. She wanted to heal. Italy became her new home and life, so she adapted to the Italian way of living—including the language. It was there that she met her second husband. He had a medical background and provided stability and a solid foundation that enabled Christine to carry on and rebuild her life.

Through her second marriage, she welcomed two wonderful children. However, still carrying her past traumas, she never taught her kids to speak German. Because of this decision, the kids could not effectively communicate with their Austrian relatives except in English—which their mother did not speak. It caused a great deal of difficulty in maintaining tightly knit family relationships.

As time went on, Christine discovered her greatest passion in horses. Horses became everything to her. They encompassed all of her love and passion, particularly when her husband began an international career that required a great deal of travel, often for weeks at a time. Horses became her sanctuary from the storm.

However, one horse turned into two horses, then three, four, five, six, and seven, until all of their money had been invested in horses. While their money was tied entirely up in horses, Christine would say it was all worth it. As she started spending more and more time with the horses, the healing process started, and slowly she recovered from many of her past traumas. She became stronger and more capable of reconnecting with her broken past. Finally, she felt capable of contacting me—her older brother—after many years. She could even visit her aging mother without getting caught up in the many tragedies of their past.

Her soul was healed of a past filled with heartache and trauma. She credits the time spent with her horses for the bulk of this transformative healing. Horses can heal the heart and soul while enabling humans to move past their tragic histories and deep hurt.

HEALING THROUGH DOGS

Leonora and Jack

Leonora has had Jack since September 2004. Back then, he was only a puppy, no more than two months old.

"After I lost my mother in January of 2014, there were days when getting up seemed unthinkable and, might I venture to say, inconsequential—but Jack didn't permit that," she said. "He depends on my significant other and me for his strolls, his food, new water, and for us to play with him."

Furthermore, because he's been visually impaired for many years now, he requires somewhat more consideration and dedication of care than other dogs. Essentially, Leonora and her partner guide Jack around the house on a case-by-case basis. For the most part, he does fine on his own. However, on occasion, he loses his focus and will stall out in the corner of a room in their home. He needs to be re-directed when this occurs. In addition, he can't simply be let out back to do his business, so they must take him on several frequent half-mile strolls to meet his bodily needs.

Leonora shared that very much as a seeing-eye dog may do for his owner, "Jack depends on us to be his eyes." As well as focusing on him every day, Leonora relied on her closeness with Jack for comfort on the numerous restless evenings that spring up during the grieving process. Feeling distraught and unable to sleep, Leonora would get on the floor with Jack after her better half fell asleep. She would put her head close to his, read a messy romance book, stroke his fur, and let the constant rhythm of his breathing quiet her down. "We did a great deal snuggling during those initial months," she recalled. "We would just stay there until I was so drained that I would slither once more into bed and, finally, nod off."

Sadness can be deadening and desolate. One of the straightforward delights is Jack. He gets energized when his pet guardians stroll in the entryway following a day at work. He wags his tail as a sign of appreciation when they feed him. He welcomes them both at the entryway at every opportunity upon their arrival home. He's calmed down significantly as he moves toward the age of twelve, but his joy is always evident.

"He'll lie with his head in my lap while I tone or read, and I realize that regardless, he cherishes me genuinely," Leonora informed me. That's how offering a dog basic reassurance helps you as a trade-off. "There were a couple of evenings where I wailed right into his fur, which I found was very spongy," she joked. "It's entertaining that I have a spouse, many important tasks, and a family that needs me," she explained, "yet in some cases, the main thing that assisted me with moving forward, slowly but surely, was my dog, Jack."

Leonora has flourished with the help of her loved ones. However, human care and support aren't needed every so often. Instead, to effectively manage pity, sadness, tension, loneliness, or other misery, you need something more than humankind can offer as comfort. The sadness alone deters you from discussing it, examining it, or in any event, mulling over everything. Sometimes talking is *not* what we need. "Sometimes," Leonora shared, "Jack lets me vibe precisely how I want, without feeling the need to present different ideas or fix the problems that surface immediately—and that is a true gift."

"I'm grateful for Jack, as he has consistently played a major role in aiding me through the most recent couple of years," Leonora admitted.

Fish

HEALING THROUGH CATS

Carlton, Dakota, and Lily—Cats for the "Non-Cat" Person

Meet Lily. She came into my life at the perfect time—after I'd encountered my own misfortune and made up for the shortcomings in my family history. However, our family story is neither here nor there—but I wouldn't trade Lily coming into my life for anything, and I have Cat's Cradle Shelter to thank for that.

From the very beginning, I've never been a "cat sweetheart." It's not that I didn't *like* cats. I had just never pondered having them. I grew up with dogs, thus accepted the idea that I'd get a dog by default and tradition. Again, this isn't to say that I despised cats. I adored pretty much all animals—but to me, cats were, indeed, just cats. I was searching for a faithful, loyal pet who needed to be with me. That didn't seem like the commonly accepted cat stereotype.

Nonetheless, that all changed when I met my better half—who preferred cats—in 2010. On the off chance that he had a pet, I knew it'd turn out to be a cat. I think he naturally realized that assuming we got a dog, he would endure most of the work. For example, he would handle all the external strolls in all sorts of weather, washroom obligations, clean-ups, and other general care, while I got to do the pleasant stuff like petting, playing, and snuggling. (This totally would have occurred. I can concede that.)

It wasn't until I observed a homeless cat wandering around near our home that I agreed to make do with a cat. I first noticed what a wonderful disposition this animal seemed to have, which came across as unusual as I generally had the feeling that cats were threatening, nasty, and aloof. Given my situation as a penniless pet person, I needed a pet that would essentially adore me regardless of my life situation. I didn't expect a cat to perform well in that capacity! Yet, this cat wasn't like that at all. He immediately approached me and let me pet and scoop him up. It was as if he genuinely just *needed* me to pet him—and I needed to pet him. It helped his case somewhat that he looked as if he was half-starved! I took him in that day.

A couple of days and one vet trip later, I discovered that he had no owner. We chose to keep him, even though he was inflicted with a terrible case of ear vermin and worms. We treated his health issues and named him Carlton. He was, presumably, the very first step toward my turning into a "cat woman." He showed me that my cat generalizations were far from exact. He's warm, loveable, and loves me unconditionally. A couple of years after bringing Carlton home, and after discovering that he absolutely HATES dogs (an alternate story by and large), I began looking at getting another cat to keep Carlton in good company. This was when Dakota came into our life.

Dakota was another "salvage" of sorts. My significant other's cousin observed a young kitten wandering in and out from a hedge outside her apartment building. Since she wasn't permitted to have pets in her loft, she called us to see if we may be interested in taking her. Dakota was little and lovable. I could not say no! All signs pointed to the fact that his mom had deserted him or that something had happened to her. Again, we took him in and headed to the vet, who assessed that he was around three weeks to about a month old.

We became hopelessly enamored with Dakota right away, even though he was not quite the same as Carlton. Carlton resembled an elderly person. He gets pleasure from snuggling with his mother, eating, resting, and indeed, that's the long and short of it. Dakota, however, got a kick out of the chance to play, eat frozen yogurt, and peer out our enormous picture window that overlooks the cherry bloom tree. After he became used to us, and when he was calm, he'd get comfortable resting on my cushion with Carlton or under our bed. For quite some time, he was a significant piece of our family.

Toward the beginning of January 2014, we woke up to Dakota scratching at the restroom entryway. He'd regularly play with my robe strings with the result of accidentally closing the entryway on himself, after which he'd emit an alarm to let us know. We got up to let him out as we'd done so many times previously. Yet, this time something was different. Something was wrong. We watched him stroll into our room, where he murmured uproariously, then fell over and died right there on our bedroom floor. We were damaged, greatly suffering from this unexpected blow, and covered under an expanse of distress. I recall little from that morning other than crying so hard it appeared as though I'd been hit right upside the head.

Dakota's demise impacted us all, particularly Carlton. After his death, I strolled into our room to observe Carlton sitting on the floor gazing at the place where Dakota had passed not long before. Frequently, Carlton yowled while meandering around the house, searching for Dakota. He would sit on my lap as I cried, grasping Dakota's collar in my clenched fist.

As time elapsed and our misery began to mend somewhat, I told my better half the time had come to embrace another cat into our lives. I realized we'd most want to take a chance on a seemingly-undesirable animal, giving it a home and a superior life. I looked on the web and visited the shelters to see whether I connected with any animals I saw. During this time, I was chatting on the telephone with a friend, another "cat woman" who acted as our reference on pet adoption applications. She mentioned Cat's Cradle Shelter. I hadn't known about them previously. However, I was interested. I completed the online adoption application, and off we went to check things out there.

After showing up at Cat's Cradle, the very first thing I noticed was that the cats weren't confined! For convenience and safety, most cat havens, sanctuaries, and shelters keep their animals in confines in varying degrees—ranging from small rooms to cages. Then, if you find an animal that you're intrigued by, you can go into a room and "play" with them to see if it is a good fit. However, in this situation, despite the cats giving off the impression of being generally well cared for, seeing them in confines is still really discouraging. It isn't easy to understand what each individual is like with them caged. However, Cat's Cradle has changed this entire concept. Cats are kept in local area rooms where you can visit with them while they meander uninhibitedly. There are rooms full of roaming cats, free to be themselves and connect with potential adopters. It's essentially a "cat woman's" fantasy!

I was searching for the "right" cat, and I knew I would know it when I came across it—or at least I hoped. I began my search in the main, largest room. As I looked around, petting the cats that passed by and calling them over, a little orange cat strolled right over to me. A volunteer let me know that her name was Bambi and that she was one of a litter of cats that was discovered behind a local Walgreens. She was still standing near me, looking inquisitively, so I scooped her up. To my great delight, she immediately snuggled her tiny face right into my shoulder, purring. My heart liquified!

Finally, I pulled myself away from Bambi to see the other rooms within Cat's Cradle. As we strolled from one space to another, playing and petting different cats, my thoughts continued to return to Bambi. After wandering the entirety of the rescue, I had no doubts whatsoever. It was Bambi. We needed her. We returned to officially adopt her the following day. The earliest trait we learned about Bambi was… Oh boy, does she HATE vehicle rides!

Carlton's interest in Bambi's arrival could only be described as "obsessed." He needed to be wherever she was. He followed her from one space to another. Unfamiliar with this bigger cat, she would dash away in fear. Yet, Carlton took it in stride and didn't surrender, regardless of the amount she smacked at his nose with her paw. His persistence paid off, and they became the best of friends after some time. On her first night in her new home, Bambi made herself at home by making her resting place directly atop her mother's—my—face. Not wanting to be impolite, I let her stay right there. Additionally, it was so adorable I couldn't help but leave her be! We changed her name to Lily and never looked back.

Cat's Cradle is genuinely astonishing. I realized the moment I strolled in that this was where I would eventually track down my new pet. The amount of love and the level of care they show their cats are immediately evident. I even witnessed a few different cats being adopted on that very day! Pets, similar to individuals, need love and trust to let their true personalities shine through. It was endearing to see these awesome individual staff members, volunteers, and adopters having an effect. While the excursion that led to us finding our Lily started with a colossal misfortune, it must have been meant to be, as she was the one that genuinely helped us mend our hearts.

All homeless pets, in shelters or on the streets, deserve to become members of a family with a permanent home—not only for the comfort of the pets—but the people who need them. There are so many pets without homes out there that I never miss an opportunity to spread the word about Cat's Cradle since they do such a fantastic job with getting these animals homes—and caring for them in the interim.

As you can see from the stories in this section, there are myriad ways that animals can forge connections and provide joy, relief, and comfort to individuals. Finding the perfect companion couldn't be easier with hundreds of thousands of pets in rescues and shelters and offers so many benefits – both to you and your furry friend.

THE HUMAN-ANIMAL BOND
THROUGH TIME

The human-animal link is defined as "a mutually beneficial and dynamic relationship between people and animals," according to the American Veterinary Medical Association (AVMA). For thousands of years, humanity has reaped the benefits of this one-of-a-kind link. Early humans relied on animals so much that there is evidence supporting the idea that we would not have survived or thrived as a species without them.

A scientific characterization of the link shared by anybody who has ever owned a pet or worked animal is unlikely. Our bonds with dogs, cats, birds, reptiles, amphibians, horses, and other pets transcend beyond words. Our pets can sense our emotions and may bring us joy and calm, rivaling even the closest human ties in our lives.

If you live in the United States, you're probably used to little (or big!) paws wandering across your bed or a cold, damp nose on your hand when you wake up. According to the American Pet Products Association's (APPA) National Pet Owners Survey from 2017–18, 68 percent of U.S. households own a pet, equating to 84.6 million households. While dogs and cats continue to be the most popular pets, horses, birds, fish, reptiles, and other animals are also popular.

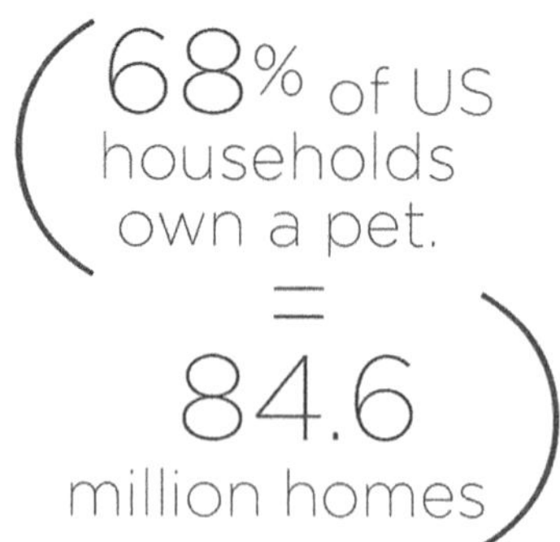

Pets are very important to Americans. According to the APPA, $72.1 billion will be spent on pets in the United States alone this year, up from $69.5 billion in 2017. Food, supplies, over-the-counter medicine, veterinarian treatment, live animal purchases, and other services are included in these costs.

It's not simply about how much money you spend. The ways that pets interact with their owners daily demonstrates the importance of their roles and how people nowadays respect their dogs as they would another human. According to the New York Times, 70 percent of pet owners sleep with their pets on occasion, 65 percent buy Christmas gifts for their pets, 23 percent prepare special meals for their pets, and 40 percent of married women say their pets provide them with more emotional support than their spouses.

This tie between dogs and their owners was not always this close or friendly. According to Bayer, a life science corporation, the human-animal connection has evolved for more than 15,000 years, but it began as a working relationship. Animals provided protection and support to humans while hunting, farming, or performing other essential duties in everyday life. Tracking and herding dogs would be used primarily. Cats traditionally lived outside and hunted and killed rodents that could spread disease or destroy food or other supplies if populations were left unchecked.

During wartime, animals were often used to help people. Cavalry horses, sentry dogs, delivery pigeons, and even mascot animals have all served in the military in the past, according to the United States Army Medical Department Journal (AMDJ). According to AMDJ, these animals could also bring stress alleviation and a sense of pride to their human counterparts, in addition to providing defense.

How the Human-Animal Bond Benefits Us

Our pets benefit from the human-animal bond in a variety of ways. We ensure that they have substantial food, water, shelter, medical treatment, amusement, and affection because we love them. However, the different ways humans benefit from the presence of their animals goes beyond the fulfillment of basic needs:

- **Stress Relief:** Petting an animal has been shown to diminish feelings of stress and pressure in people.

- **Improved Autonomy and Healing:** Service and therapy animals are priceless to their handlers. They assist in everyday errands, allowing for increased levels of autonomy. In addition, they provide mental support after trauma and aid in recovery from horrendous mishaps. Service animals help people overcome both physical and mental challenges.

- **Improved State of Mind:** Studies show that the straightforward demonstration of stroking a well-disposed animal expands dopamine and serotonin levels in the cerebrum, two synthetic substances that are fundamental for joy and unwinding.

- **Increased Activity Through Responsibility:** The responsibility of caring for a pet requires a significant level of work, leading to increased activity levels. Living with a pet that needs a daily (or more frequent) walk or play session is a fantastic method for getting off the sofa and out the door. Walking out of the house is the most challenging part!

- **Improved Resilience to Respiratory and Allergy Ailments:** Children who grow up with animals exhibit fewer allergic sensitivities and are less likely to be diagnosed with asthma than those who aren't raised with animals.

- **Social Associations:** Thanks to their care requirements, pets furnish us with various opportunities to get out and communicate with our companions and neighbors. This is particularly useful for seniors or others who might be more averse to incorporating social action into their day-to-day routines.

- **Basic Reassurances:** Your pet doesn't care about how much money you make, what sort of vehicle you drive, what you look like, or whether or not you wear name-brand garments. Pets furnish us with fair, unlimited encouragement and love. These are essential reassurances we all need, and pets offer them freely.

PETS, HUMANS, AND THEIR HEALTH

It is easy to overlook the human-animal bond as a one-way street. Pets need their owners to meet their basic needs of food, water, shelter, and welfare. However, it is crucial to remember that humans can gain a different kind of well-being from their companion animals. Research shows that pets can lower blood pressure, reduce stress, raise blood oxytocin levels, and, in some cases, reduce direct pain. According to Bayer, people living with dogs are fifteen percent less likely to die from heart disease.

Pets also can offer benefits for other human health challenges as well. The elderly respond particularly well to companion animals. According to Bayer, diseases like depression, coronary conditions, and dementia can be exacerbated by loneliness. Seniors can experience positive mental and physical effects by interacting with companion animals. Similar results have been shown to occur in children during emotional, cognitive, social, and behavioral development.

Today's Working and Production Animals
The human-animal bond is not only between ordinary pets and their owners but can be seen in an assortment of other

settings. In particular, working animals are known for their associations with their human overseers. Emotional support, service, treatment, and therapy animals provide solace, offer security, and perform day-to-day undertakings to help their owners manage their lives more independently. Animals can be a significant piece of the recovery system for individuals who experience physical and mental injuries, including veterans who have served during wartime.

Animals can offer different types of assistance, as well. Ranchers have been known to station peacocks to look after their property and domesticated animals. Law enforcement organizations rely upon dogs to track and catch suspects and distinguish bombs and opiates from other substances. The U.S. Navy's battle dolphins identify submerged mines and the presence of foe swimmers or submersibles. At the same time, the Marines have involved donkeys in an assortment of their missions by charging them with moving weapons, ammo, and other supplies through troublesome landscapes.

Ranchers, farmers, overseers, and veterinarians foster unique bonds with the domesticated animals under their care. While different from that of the typical pet owner, this bond is similarly solid and is tied to human sympathy. Tending to the animals gives them a sense of satisfaction.

The Human-Animal Bond of the Future
As the human-animal bond has advanced throughout time, we can only imagine that it will continue developing and creating new connections between individuals and various animals. The medical advantages of training service animals and cooperating with several types of working animals are already

well-documented and have significant effects on the existence of many individuals.

As this bond continues to grow and fortify, human beings will likely focus on new areas of wellbeing that animals can help us better manage. We will learn to rely on animals in new ways. We can only assume that as veterinarians and scientists explore more deeply into the realm of human-animal bonds and the ever-changing farming industry continues to shift, new exploration and conventions will alter the connections among people and animals.

This is particularly evident when examined in the context of One Health, an idea that portrays the wellbeing of people, animals, ecosystems, and climate are forever and inextricably integrated. While a large part of past discussion and momentum in connection with the One Health idea fixates on zoonotic infection and disease transfer, there is much more to it than that. Many more links can be made between the pillars of health, such as the connection between humans and our domesticated pets—and their critical roles in ensuring our physical, mental, and cultural wellbeing. It is clear that the health of humans is, more and more, being seen as interconnected with the presence and wellbeing of their pets. As researchers continue to acquire information about the medical advantages of the human-animal bond, we can only assume that this bond will keep on evolving.

COMPANION ANIMALS AND SPIRITUALITY

Companion animals. We choose to bring them into our life at times. They occasionally wander in and never leave. They quickly take over your life in ways that someone who has never had a companion animal may find difficult to understand. We certainly cannot put it into mere words.

Companion animals, defined as "those animals we invite into our homes, lives, and hearts," may have no practical or economic purpose in urban life and might even put a financial strain on their human caregivers. Despite this, companion animals are found in 62% of Australian households, and there are more companion animals in Australia than humans. So, why do so many people form such a profound and lasting bond with their animal companions?

For decades, studies have repeatedly documented the physical, emotional, and social benefits that some people gain from living with and caring for a companion animal. The physical benefits of dogs and the necessity to walk them (regardless of the weather) are self-evident. But what about the rest? Cleaning up dirty paw prints; changing litter trays or bedding; sweeping up countless dust balls clumped together with cat or dog hair, feathers, or seed husks; or responding to their urgent need to eat—or toilet—every time you think it is safe to sit down or sleep in! Despite the additional strain they may put on our households, we love our pets because they contribute an overwhelming amount of goodness to our lives.

The psychological advantages are apparent. Animals are selfless in their love. A gentle head butt, a tail wag, a purr, or an adoring lick originate from the heart. For many people, nurturing the source of this unconditional love can provide a meaningful purpose in life. Whenever a human gazes at their beloved companion animal, the very same hormones that bind a mother and newborn to each other are released. Soon, the relationship is unshakable, and you will drag yourself out of bed in the morning to care for your animal companion's needs, regardless of how you feel or how bad the weather is.

In terms of social contact, research consistently shows that animals serve as a conduit for human interaction. All types of pets allow for sharing animal-related anecdotes and admittance into a group of like-minded people who are bonded by their love and affection for animals. At the same time, dog walking can be a terrific way to meet new people. There are photos to share and debates to have about cuteness levels, incredibly comical pet antics, and even eating and toileting routines. People are more than twice as likely to share images of their cat on social media as they are to upload pictures of themselves, according to an industry study.

Connection to a friendly animal can likewise bring heartache. Over twenty years of examining the ramifications of friend-animal loss consistently reveal that the feelings of loss experienced when a pet passes are proportionate to those felt when experiencing the loss of a human connection. Nonetheless, an individual's enthusiastic, mental, physical, and profound reaction to losing their adored animal buddy may not be completely perceived by those around them, implying that the connections between humans and animals are not as deep as those between humans. In this time of despondency, the otherworldly association between human and animal is regularly referenced, and the need to maintain bonds with the perished friend-animal is revealed.

For certain individuals, the otherworldly association between humans and animals begins long before the animal's passing. This was particularly obvious in a progression of meetings I directed among animal lovers whose life directions had been fundamentally changed by a progression of unexpected events. While portraying his cherished maturing dog, interviewee 'Robbie' remarked:

I'm sure he's a part of me, part of my soul, my best mate. I know he's old, but if possible, I love him even more for being old. He's taught me not to fear death. He's not scared, and he's not even bothered about getting old, he just accepts and keeps loving.

A Spiritual Connection

Since the beginning of humanity and across societies, animals have co-habited with people. Archeological records show animals included in the craftsmanship, engineering, fables, and strict otherworldly customs of numerous ancient cultures (Wilmer, 2019). Additionally, animal images and illustrations have shown up across vast geological areas, and animal gatekeeper spirits were frequently called upon to intercede with helping humans to recuperate and achieve prosperity.

Given this historical record and the solid friendships that we all know tie humans to animals, it is to be expected that certain individuals will feel a profound bond with their pets. Otherworldliness can be a troublesome idea to characterize, yet there are a few critical parts detailed in the accompanying definition:

Otherworldliness is the part of humankind that alludes to how people look for and express importance and reason and how they experience their connectedness to events, themselves, other people, nature, and the spiritual. Otherworldliness supports relationship-focused consideration and is firmly connected to an individual's feeling of direction and association, ideas that are reliably included in human-animal writing.

Animals are additionally all-around situated to provide a channel to the regular world, subsequently working with a connectedness to nature that can be absent in the lives of many individuals. Drawing on the meaning of otherworldliness, the human-animal bond and otherworldliness can be analyzed in three center spaces: animals as a channel to the regular world; animals and non-verbal connectedness to a guiltless awareness; and animals as a blissful association with the occasion.

Connection to the Natural World

During the 1950s, German logician, psychoanalyst, and social therapist, Erich Fromm, composed mankind's 'Existential Division,' which emerged from the idea of being important for nature yet rising above it through the advancement of mindfulness and reason. A few accepted that the more individuals were isolated from the natural world, the more critical the need was to get away from this separation and resulting feelings of pointlessness.

Pediatric clinician Boris Levinson regularly referred to as the originator of animal-assisted treatment, agreed with Fromm's thoughts about human separation from the natural world. He expressed, "One of the main purposes behind men's present troubles is his failure to deal with his internal identity and to harmonize his way of life with his enrollment in the realm of nature."

These convictions were formalized in E.O. Wilson's (1984) 'Biophilia Speculation,' which depicts the transformative significance of humankind's need to comprehend and live together within the natural world as both hunter and prey. While direct reliance on nature for actual survival has been diminished for some urban-dwelling people, there remains an essential need in the human mind to keep up with or restore an association with nature. For certain individuals, pets can provide a channel to mindful attention concerning the steady impacts of the natural world, thereby restoring a connectedness with the vastness of nature.

Extensive research and study reliably support the calming and healing properties of maintaining relationships with dogs, cats, horses, birds, and other living animals. It is effective regardless of whether this is accomplished by looking into an aquarium, stroking a purring cat, or essentially losing oneself in the experience of associating with a conscious being who is naturally receptive to familiar non-verbal correspondence. In this manner, connectedness to an animal can go past the delight of association with the world to the shared delight of implicit love and affection.

Non-Verbal Connectedness to an Innocent Sentient Being
In 2012, a conspicuous gathering of researchers marked the Cambridge Declaration of Consciousness, which confirmed that people are not extraordinary in having portions of the mind that produce a mindful state. Countless non-human animals, including warm-blooded animals and birds, are conscious; they experience what is befalling them and have positive and negative conditions, including dread, play, humiliation, outrage, aggravation, love, misery, and melancholy.

This endorsement of the view that animals can 'feel feelings' presumably did not shock the many animal lovers who had previously anthropomorphized their dearest pets. Humanoid attribution, which is characterized as the 'attribution of human mental states (considerations, sentiments, inspirations, and convictions) to nonhuman animals,' is common among individuals with regard to their pets. Individuals give their animals human names, chat for their sake, celebrate their birthdays, and lament with a deep sense of grief when they pass away.

In reflecting upon the personalities of animals, Mark Bekoff—a supporter of the Cambridge Declaration and prestigious for his active interest in animal conduct, mental ethology (the investigation of animal minds), and merciful protection—remarked on the profound significance of observing the hallowed connections between individual animals and humans. Discussing his own dearest German Shepherd, Jethro, Bekofff portrayed that it is a miracle in friendship that such close links between human beings and other living animals can rise out of the human-animal bond. He accepted that there were types of correspondence and shared inclination, animal-to-animal, that led to the immediate knowledge of precisely what the other species was feeling and attempting to say.

This implicit correspondence and feelings of marvel were evident when I spoke with the gathering of animal lovers on the importance of their relationship with their pets. As 'Vince' clarified:

I realized the animals improved my life and mended pieces of my mind. I believe it's the completeness, that culmination. It's the actual material sensation combined with that enthusiastic reaction. On top of that, there's an otherworldly association, that mystic holding. It's implicit. Words aren't required. Something occurs. It's truly significant–it's that feeling of unity–and I can fail to remember all the not-super great pieces of my life.

Another interviewee 'Joe,' who became progressively housebound as his health declined, portrayed the relationship he imparted to a bird:

It's weird, yet I, in all actuality, do feel in a profound way leaned towards him. There's this inferred stuff that goes on constantly between us. There'll be a touch, a look, a moan. It resembles an implicit language, so I think, comprehensively, we're totally in order. I know we're an odd couple. However, I believe we're likewise similar to perfect partners.

The miracle of friendship and profound improvement inside the human-animal relationship can ground an individual immovably in the present time and place.

Living in the Moment

Encountering a connectedness to events, self, and others is key to otherworldliness, and animals have an extraordinary method of taking individuals back to the current occasion. Individuals characterize their animal partners as relatives, with the animal regularly considered much like a small child. Exhibiting attributes such as being perky, lively, inquisitive, adorable, and loving inspires sensations of euphoria and nurturance in adults. Like a child, animals exhibit the capacity to live in the now through games played with human companions in the moment.

Formative analyst and psychoanalyst Erik Erikson remarked that an individual ought to reestablish a portion of the fun-loving nature of their youth at each phase of the grown-up life cycle. For Erikson, play equated to aliveness, representing something with no end, and personally connected to an imperative contribution throughout everyday life. Joy.

The significant association between play and living in the present time and place was featured by 'Brenton' while clarifying his relationship with Tom, the cat.

In any case, we've shared a lot, and he has a universal knowledge of me. He brought the fun back into my life when I thought it was gone for eternity. I can watch him playing in a vacant box or with a crumpled-up piece of paper, and for that short time frame, I'm living at that time, with no previous or second thoughts and no considerations of things to come.

Cats have a long history with people, with the most distant archeological proof of cats and humans dwelling together going back 9,500 years to Cyprus. This was during the human progress to agribusiness—and it occurred thanks to the need to control vermin. While cats may not act merely as vermin control in most families today, their casual, somewhat standoffish, yet charming persona has seen them become solidly settled in living souls. With their high-level mental capacity, people can think about existential nervousness, yet cats (and many different animals) remain grounded in the moment, giving forth a connectedness to the self and otherworldliness.

Final Thoughts

Pets. We bring them into our lives, our homes, and our hearts. We tidy up after them, excuse their occasionally humiliating propensities, and, when necessary, we manage to cover their veterinary expenses. In any case, the profound bond with our pets is unadulterated and honest, a cushion to regular stressors and fundamentally human feelings of dread of partition and relinquishment. Each time you love an animal, talk about their assumed thoughts, chuckle at their shenanigans, or lament their demise, you are producing a consecrated security.

Remember this… The dog and cat hairs that decorate all your garments are respectable symbols. The sloppy paw prints and scratched furniture are a direction for living that changes your house into a 'home.' What's more is that every time you ponder the delight and marvel at your astonishing animal friend, you are sharing a snapshot of spiritual communication.

BEHAVIORAL TRAITS OF PETS AND HUMANS

Many studies have uncovered that pets and their owners share a significant number of similar character traits. This peculiarity could be caused by the everyday encounters shared by people and their cherished animals. Or, perhaps, it is because individuals are attracted to pets that they feel look and act like themselves.

"Given the tight mental associations among individuals and their pets, almost certainly, dogs and cats are fit to various human characters," said University of Texas clinician Sam Gosling. In 2010, Gosling utilized a web-based review to examine the qualities of individuals who recognize themselves as being either dog individuals or cat individuals. In connection with the survey of 4,565 people, Gosling concluded that "there is truth to the broadly held view that, as a rule, the characters of dog individuals contrast from those of cat individuals."

Curiously, the typical character attributes of animal people were viewed as very near to those seen in the real world. For instance, dog individuals were more outgoing, agreeable, compassionate, and insightful. Cat individuals were viewed as more masochistic, judgemental, and more manipulative. In any case, the study's results uncovered that cat individuals were more daring and offbeat than dog individuals.

Dr. Stanley Coren published his results and detailed these discoveries in Psychology Today. Gosling's work was centered around the Big Five character attributes: extroversion, agreeableness, openness, conscientiousness, and neuroticism. Dr. Coren utilized the Interpersonal Adjective Scale to analyze the social propensities of animal people. He noted likenesses in the discoveries of the two studies.

"The overall example that emerges from the two studies is that dog owners are more friendly, intuitive, and tolerating, and cat owners are more withdrawn, independent, and less amiable," composed Dr. Coren.

Recently, analysts at Michigan State University surveyed the owners of 1,600 dogs, including 50 unique varieties. The pet people portrayed their character traits and personalities just the same as the characteristics and behavior of their dogs. The analysts found that dog characteristics change over the long run and are affected by their ways of life and encounters as they become older.

"Very much like people, dogs fluctuate in their characteristics. Also, they might conceivably change after some time. The dog you bring home from the shelter isn't going to be at all similar to the one you'll have a long time from now," said lead creator William Chopik.

The study also uncovered that dog and owner characteristics regularly reflect one another. Restless or forceful dogs were found to ordinarily have owners who exhibited pessimistic characteristics, while dynamic and active dogs had owners who acted the same way. Chopik clarified that either individuals are most likely to select dogs that match their ways of life or that dog and human characteristics converge over the long term because of shared ways of life.

Clinician Richard Wiseman additionally investigated the personality qualities of pets and their owners. He noted undeniable contrasts among the pet owners of different species. "Fish owners were the most joyful, dog owners the most enjoyable to be with, cat owners the most trustworthy and sincerely delicate, and reptile owners the most free."

We, people, are a perplexing pack, and our choices of which pets to provide homes to adds just one more layer to the many intricate components of our personalities.

Think about it. Why do you think your friend may lean towards keeping a cat as a pet while your immediate inclination is to bring home a dog? Why do some get a kick out of the opportunity to keep reptiles at home as their pets? Could we, by chance, see ourselves in our pets?

For this analysis, we investigated information from various studies. We likewise inspected why we keep pets. Interestingly, it appears as though we're the only species of the world that, collectively, keeps pets of another species and fabricates long-term connections with them.

We wanted to investigate pet ownership all over the planet to uncover what being a dog-, cat-, or even fish-person could reveal about you. Before you wail (or whimper!) in complaint as you review this information, consider that these conclusions were more casually-drawn rather than logical!

How Do People Describe Their Furry Friends?

The information provided by pet owners indicates that most American pets are more amicable than modest (half versus 42%), more tenacious than standoffish (half versus 35%), more trusting than dubious (57% versus 31%), and more hyperactive than lethargic (51% versus 30%).

However, life as a pet isn't consistently daylight and treats. Three out of 10 respondents concede their pets are "restless," while another 33% would depict their pet as a "busybody." One of every five think their pet is downright strange, and another 48% say they've seen their pet participate in conduct that is considered surprising for their size or species. This includes cats who play fetch or giant dogs that lie across individuals' legs like little lap dogs. Almost six out of 10 (57%) say their pets act differently when they believe they're not being watched.

"My present dog will attempt to gradually remove things from the rubbish when she believes I'm not looking," one respondent tells the survey. Another pet owner reports that they've caught their pet "licking a table leg in the family room."

"In any event, when we're not investing quite a lot more energy at home, we as a whole love recounting tales about our pets," says Zippy Paws Co-Founder Jen Glaser. "Furthermore, with the ascent of remote work, we're currently ready to notice them during parts of the day they used to have all to themselves, so it's nothing unexpected that we feel more on top of their characters than any other time in recent memory."

Pet Owners Can Read Their Companion Like a Book
Out of the 57% of respondents who own various pets, 80% say they generally know which one is making a commotion in another room even when they aren't looking. Three of every four respondents (76%) even say they can generally determine what their pet is thinking just from their overall expressions and body language.

In any case, knowing your pet in such a detailed way doesn't mean you always realize what they will like. Indeed, 80% of Americans have purchased their pet a unique bed to make them comfortable, yet just 58% say their pet utilizes it.

"The stuff we purchase for our pet sometimes says more about us as it does about them," Glaser states. "You may purchase a toy formed like a jug of rosé because it's your favorite wine; however, your dog only knows that it's amusing to bite on!"

Every breed has qualities that set it apart from others. For example, Labrador dogs and Ragdoll cats are laid-back animals, but Abyssinian cats and Australian Shepherd dogs are more high-maintenance and high-strung. In terms of being overweight, Sphinx cats and Beagles come in first and second, confirming their image as foodies. Aside from the breed itself, a variety of additional factors have an impact on your pet's emotional and physical well-being.

Mental Health – Yours and Your Pet's

Mental health is a topic that has recently gained attention in the media, and as we've discussed, pets can help improve our mental health. But did you realize that it also pertains to our pets? Pet personalities, like their human counterparts, are vulnerable to change over time, according to a Michigan State University study. Changes in your life impact your pet, just as they do on you. According to the study, adopted shelter pets who showed signs of anxiety and aggression may have a harder time adjusting when their owner is equally high strung.

Further, the study found that anxious/aggressive owners had more anxious/aggressive dogs in social circumstances. In contrast, extroverted people raised more exuberant and active dogs, and quieter, calmer people raised easy-going dogs.

Physical Health Implications

Looking more deeply into the impacts of owner characteristics and their influence on pets, a report by analysts from the University of Lincoln and Nottingham Trent University in the United Kingdom showed that the human character significantly influences their idea of appropriate care of their pets.

Owner character was separated into five character traits: Agreeableness, Conscientiousness, Extroversion, Neuroticism, and Openness. Every owner shared data about their cats' physical wellbeing, breed, conduct attributes, and what the cat's life was like overall. After assessing more than 3,000 responses, the researchers drew connections between the owner's character and the potential for medical conditions to develop in the cat. Those owners who scored higher on the neuroticism scale would generally have indoor cats who showed anxiety-related sicknesses, continuous physical ailments, and an inclination to be overweight.

Outgoing owners would, in general, permit their cat to approach the outside, while more introverted owners noted cats with restlessness and stress-related diseases.

What Does It Mean For You?

As a pet owner, you can certainly take a step back and evaluate how your animal's personality relates to your own. Once you do, you may discover that you become more conscious of your habits – or at least aware of their consequences.

Look to the Owner

To understand that a pet owner can impact how their pets are seen and the sort of life they experience, those who own or work with these animals should have at least a basic comprehension of human brain research.

Conduct change is frequently the first and primary sign that an animal is unwell physically or mentally. One of the most noteworthy parts of an animal's case history is the changes in behavior that owners report. The quality and exactness of this data from owners on their pets are critical. In any case, this data is subjective and might be firmly affected by the relationship that owners have with their pets or impacted by the past experiences of that pet owner.

This proof that owner attributes might impact numerous parts of their pet's life—including possibly how the pet presents to a veterinary facility—prompts us to consider how to use this information to improve behaviors and other issues. Incorporating video records of the animal's unwanted behavior for clinical conduct or behavioral cases is essential. Owners are now very skilled at catching and providing video proof of specific activities to their veterinarians—and it can be extremely valuable.

There are many different methods and tools that enable pet owners and handlers to monitor and record information about behavior. Some of these methods rely on app technology, for example, "dog logbooks." These applications enjoy the benefit of portability, ease of use, and the inclusion of a period/date stamp that can assist with keeping an ordered record of the pet owner's observations and perceptions.

A Complex Relationship

Owner-veterinarian relationships take a long time to develop, and even once they are firmly established, they can be exceedingly complicated. A veterinarian who is familiar with both the owner and the pet will recognize minor clinical symptoms that would otherwise be overlooked. However, each clinical situation must be interpreted in light of the human baggage that accompanies it into the consultation room.

It's all too easy to overlook the importance of the owner's personality in their interactions with their pet and how that personality may influence how they view the animals, manage them, and care for their health.

DOGS AND THEIR OWNERS SHARE SIMILAR PERSONALITY TRAITS

Our relationships with dogs have changed drastically over time. However, humans have chosen to intimately share their lives with their companion dogs in recent times. This has been all-around beneficial to both species. Now, we typically see better treatment of dogs, a more thorough comprehension of the species overall by specialists, and better medical services are available for these animals.

"When people face significant changes throughout everyday life, their character traits can change in accompaniment with this. We observed that this also occurs with dogs, and in surprisingly consistent and powerful ways," said lead creator Professor William Chopik. "We anticipated that the dogs' characters should be genuinely steady since they don't have to deal with the number or chaos of life changes most people do, yet we learned that they do, in fact, change a great deal. We revealed similarities to their owners, the ideal time frame for training, and surprisingly, that there is a period in their lives that they can get more forceful toward different animals."

The specialists also observed that a dog's character could anticipate and respond to numerous significant life changes by shifting traits such as how close they become with their owners, their gnawing conduct, and how they process any ongoing ailments. In a review distributed in Applied Animal Behavior Science, specialists requested that pet guardians rate themselves on five significant character aspects. The Big Five, as they're alluded to in psychology and brain research, are:

- Neuroticism (a tendency towards anxiety and fear)
- Extraversion
- Conscientiousness
- Agreeableness
- Openness (level of creativity, curiosity, and being open to new ideas)

Pet guardians predominantly responded that they share every one of the Big Five character aspects with their dogs. To be certain the outcomes weren't simple projections created by pet guardians; unbiased companions were additionally surveyed about the dog and human pairs. They also evaluated them as sharing every one of the aspects, aside from receptiveness.

The inquiries to the people participating in the study covered various qualities. Every member considered their personal characteristics across general classifications, such as whether they are independent or outgoing or open to new experiences. The dog portion of the study requested data about teachability, dread, connection, and the dog's responses to their owners, outsiders, and different dogs.

Of the 131 dog and human sets who began the study, 75 completed it. From the information provided, analysts found that alongside factors like age, sex, and size, owner character influenced how well the dogs responded to social adjustment. While there are a few constraints to the study—including the low number of participants in the sample group and uncontrolled factors like socialization and training history—several intriguing trends surfaced.

Interestingly, the dogs with withdrawn versus outgoing pet guardians appeared to move through the behavior portion of their training program very differently. While outgoing owners were bound to see a reduction in dogs' behavior issues, this was less true of more introverted owners.

The study also reported that outgoing individuals might have received these results due to their propensity to be "excited, receptive to social improvements, and to expose their pet to many social connections." In contrast, more introspective individuals might have been more restrained, less inclined to seek out social connections, and subsequently more anxious to open doors to socialization with others.

It was also revealed that owners who seemed more outgoing noted lower levels of fear from their dogs after the program was finished. The ability to attempt new things, they believe, may have led these pet guardians to utilize present-day training belief systems and devices before partaking in the study, such as positive reinforcement strategies like clicker training. Dog owners who scored lower might, instead, have depended on obsolete training strategies like power and discipline, which have been connected to increased fear in dogs.

Regardless of your character idiosyncrasies, resources are available to help you and your dog learn good behavior together.

Dog conduct specialists like trainers, dog conduct advisors, or guaranteed proficient dog mentors can help you and your dog establish a training plan based on positive reinforcement that will help the two of you explore the world securely together.

Why is Dog Personality Linked to Human Personality?

One possible reason dog conduct and character are so dramatically interwoven with their people is that individuals may be inclined to choose animals who reflect and supplement their own lives. A quiet human will regularly pick a calm dog. In contrast, a restless individual will embrace an anxious dog, for instance, according to Jenn Fiendish, a veterinary behavior specialist who runs Happy Power Behavior and Training in Portland, Oregon. She firmly believes that individuals do this on a subconscious level.

"When my significant other and I went to get our new dog twelve years ago, I quickly picked the pet who seemed more dynamic, scrappy, and somewhat nervous of things, which is similar to my character. My significant other picked the laid-back, quiet, and not-troubled-by-things pup, an ideal counterpart for his character. This, likewise, occurred with our other two dogs, both of whom I selected because they were spunky and somewhat wild (me again!)." She says that the dogs have kept up with, and surprisingly fortified, a significant portion of these shared characteristics through the years.

Dog Emotions Mirror Human Emotions

Considering that individuals and dogs have shared close relationships for around fifteen thousand years—researchers continue to debate this timetable—it's not unexpected that dog character has been affected.

Beastly says that dogs can observe and match human feelings. "At the point when an individual is extremely restless, our dogs get this and frequently become restless too. Assuming that the uneasiness is ongoing, the dog may likewise foster constant nervousness," she says.

Dr. Mahaney has also seen this in his training. "I have noticed pets in families where the owners are under a great deal of pressure [who will] accordingly display behavior issues which could be ascribed to the owners' absence of calming energy." A significant portion of the behavioral issues he sees include improper urination and defecation practices, causing damage to owners' property, barking and crying, and a diminished sense of hunger.

Dogs are true empaths, says Dr. Lisa Pinn McFaddin. According to Dr. McFaddin, the stronger the human-animal bond, the stronger the response. "Dogs frequently try to console and calm their unhappy people. People may not identify these efforts because they are subtle: sleeping close to the person, placing their head on the person's leg, establishing physical contact with the person, or attempting to distract the person with a toy."

Can a Dog's Personality Rub Off on Humans?

While experts say dogs are more likely to pick up personality traits from their pet parents, Dr. McFaddin believes that dog emotions and behavior can also affect humans. "I most often witness this when people's own dogs are innately apprehensive," Dr. McFaddin says. Anxiety in the dog frequently causes anxiety in the owner. The owner feels powerless to change their pet's worrying behavior. This feeling of helplessness makes the owner feel uneasy, vulnerable, and anxious as well."

Dr. McFaddin explains that physical indications and behaviors that a nervous dog could exhibit, such as panting, whining, pacing, destruction of belongings, and persistent barking, can overstimulate a pet parent.

"The owner's lifestyle becomes irritated and disrupted by the frequent movement and noise, which generates worry." On the other hand, certain incredibly quiet dogs (I call them Buddha dogs) aid in the relaxation of their owners. "The dog's intrinsic peace is physically and emotionally contagious," she adds.

"Numerous studies have indicated a reduction in anxiety, a slowing of heart rate, a lowering of blood pressure, and an increase in the production of calming hormones and neurotransmitters in both humans and dogs following positive encounters, mainly after petting," adds Dr. McFaddin. As a result, it appears that the human-animal bond benefits both sides.

Why Do Dogs Like to Cuddle?
"Dogs nestle to get warmth, bond with their relatives or pack, and because it discharges internal hormones and chemicals that cause them to feel better," Bernal says. "When dogs nestle with us, their cerebrums discharge the chemical oxytocin, which builds up their craving for and pleasure they get from close contact and holding," she adds.

The craving to snuggle is established through training and forming a close bond with a dog; however, it also connects to dogs who lived in packs before they became so interconnected with humans. Long before dogs became "man's best friend," they had developed a longing to be part of a herd made up of other dogs.

"Dogs in the wild and young puppies regularly snuggle with their littermates and mom as a method of showing submission," explained Chyrle Bonk, a veterinarian at Hepper. "When your dog nestles with you, they're showing their total trust and love in your relationship," Bonk adds.

"Dogs are pack animals naturally, so contact and friendship are a solid main avenue for affection," Bernal clarifies further. In any case, snuggles can mean different things to dogs than people, she adds. It can even prompt another typical dog behavior: Zoomies.

"For certain dogs, particularly the individuals who are more youthful and figuring out how to play, snuggling can be a method of commitment that energizes them, prompting a time of hyperactivity or those exemplary zoomies around your home," Bernal adds.

Affection can likewise transform into animosity, assuming someone else is close and the dog feels defensive of their pet parent. Owners should focus on their dog's non-verbal communication to survey whether and how they need to be snuggled.

How Do Dogs Like to Cuddle?
There are likely a similar number of types of snuggling as there are kinds of dogs on the planet: embracing, haunch scratches, ear scratching, petting, supporting your dog's face... the list continues.

"Dogs like to be nestled in various ways. Some like to cuddle on your lap, while others need to stay away a little more, yet will permit belly rubs or ear scratches," Bonk says.

Your dog's solace needs to take first concern over your destitution. "If you want your dog to be in your lap, get down to their level and sit on the floor with them," Bonk says. "Try not to compel your pet into a place that makes them uncomfortable and watch for any indications of straining or shits of their ears to know whether they're not into it."

By and large, your dog's body language can assist with directing your connection. "A few dogs will turn over on their back to request a midsection rub, and some will keep their belly completely protected and just request their back or ears to be pet," Bonk clarifies.

As you foster a bond with your dog over the long haul of pet ownership, you'll get to know their favorite types of snuggling and their ideal positions for warmth. A few dogs might like nestling, so on the off chance that you're perched on the lounge chair, they'll search out "a delicate touch by setting their head on your thigh," Bernal says. Other dogs may excitedly roll over as you stroll past, potentially showing they need a tummy rub.

To begin to learn about a pet's preferences, try not to pet a dog's head first. Instead, start with the chest area. "As a general rule, most dogs would rather not be reached over their head to be pet on the highest point on their body, as this might feel too dominant. Petting the chest might be a much better place to start," Katherine Pankratz, a board-guaranteed veterinary behaviorist, tells Inverse.

However, before getting too involved in determining how a dog most likes to be pet or snuggled, we ought to scrutinize the possibility that all dogs generally need to be cuddled in this way. "A dog's eagerness to snuggle relies extensively upon their character. Some prefer to do it more than others," Bonk says.

"Indeed, even dogs that like this type of attention probably shouldn't be subjected to it constantly," Pankratz adds. "Snuggling can be pleasant for dogs—considerably more so assuming that they can have a feeling of decision and control."

How Do You Know if Your Dog Wants to be Cuddled?

Various studies have confirmed that not only do people like to snuggle dogs but that they also receive psychological wellness benefits from petting and playing with their dog companions. Be that as it may, it's not in every case clear whether dogs have any sort of physical need to be snuggled. Stanley Coren, an expert in dog brain research, looked at photographs accessible online of individuals embracing their dogs to survey the dogs' non-verbal communication signs. As Coren reports in Psychology Today, 81.6 percent of the pictures showed dogs encountering inconvenience, stress, and tension.

This corresponds with past research showing people, particularly small kids, are awful at deciphering dog non-verbal communication, prompting possibly risky connections. A recent report observed that 53% of three-year-old children mixed up forceful dog conduct as a sign of a cheerful dog.

"Having a decent comprehension of your dog's non-verbal communication and a decent capacity likewise to assess your surroundings is vital to determining what your dog's response to different types of affection will be," Bernal says.

Here are a few rules of thumb to keep in mind:

1. **Let the dog come to you or ask for its owner's permission.** "Dogs will come directly to you or stay around when you come to them to tell you they want to be cuddled," Bonk explains.

Pankratz says it's critical to let it make the first move if you're unfamiliar with the dog. "First and foremost, obtain permission from the dog's owner to approach and communicate with their dog," Pankratz advises.

2. Assess the dog's body language.
"Understanding the indicators that a dog is eager or not so enthused for snuggling time requires reading a dog's behavior," Bernal explains. The following body language signs could suggest that a dog is friendly to other animals:

- Tail wagging
- Eye contact
- Rolling over
- Maneuvering its head, paw, or body into your personal space

"Some pups even offer their pet parent a friendly paw nudge or a mild, playful conversation to let them know they want more of those lovely pats," Bernal explains. However, some of these behaviors are easy to misread.

A wagging tail, according to Pankratz, indicates that the dog is emotional and wants to move forward—it could be happy or afraid, depending on the situation. "Facial traits and body position are more important than the tail in determining a dog's emotional condition," Pankratz explains.

Please be aware of indicators that a dog is stressed and give them space. These are some of the warning signs:

- Grumbling growl
- Baring teeth or snarling

- Tensing up
- Pinning their ears
- Shifting their weight
- Keeping their distance

Be extra cautious when it comes to dogs you've never met before. Extending a hand to a strange dog can be a reflex for dog lovers, but it's a risky move.

Pankratz explains, "You've stretched your hand into the dog's area, sometimes without completely analyzing their comfort or agreement to the interaction. An alternative technique would be to approach at a distance from the dog in a nonthreatening manner—typically turned to the side and bent down," she says. Instead of staring straight ahead, bend your head slightly to the right. Similarly, instead of extending your hand, keep it close to your body so that a dog can sniff or touch it.

These actions may indicate that an unfamiliar dog is willing to interact with you:

- Mouth hanging open softly
- Approaching with a loose, wiggly posture or leaning into you
- Soft muscles in the face or relaxed eyes

3. **Decide if the dog likes the cuddle—and re-assess.**

The dog might have acknowledged your affection; however, you need to focus on their non-verbal communication to check whether the dog's signals are pleasant or troubling.

"If their eyelids are hanging in a condition of delight, their body is loose and formed into yours; then, at that point, it is one can assume they are content," Bernal says. "If they are tense, apprehensive, or giving indications of hostility with a protesting snarl or visual appearance of their teeth, then, at that point, there might be some interaction which they are stressed over," she clarifies.

A pet resembles a handshake: You want to peruse non-verbal communication to end the handshake at the most appropriate second and continue onward. Assuming you don't, it can get awkward. The equivalent goes for dog snuggles. Petting assent tests can assist with measuring a dog's reaction, as well, Pankratz says.

All you want to accomplish for the test is to:
- Interact with the dog
- Stop
- See what they do next

A "yes" would be demonstrated by an evident willingness to interact with you again. For example, the dog may draw closer, lean on you, or rub against you. A "no" could be expressed by the dog moving away or remaining stationary. According to experts, knowing when your dog needs to be alone is just as vital as learning when they want to be cuddled.

Which Dog Breeds Like to Cuddle?
Each dog, like every human, has its own life experiences and preferences. However, one element that influences how friendly a dog is with humans is genetics.

"Aside from breeds, many other elements, such as early life experience and socialization, exposure to continuous learning experiences, and physical health, might influence whether or not a dog prefers to cuddle," Pankratz notes. It's also worth noting that, according to Pankratz, there aren't any peer-reviewed studies that compare how cuddly different dog breeds are. According to the experts, some dog breeds are considered more affectionate based on anecdotal evidence from owners over time.

"Because they're too big to be lap dogs, some of the most affectionate breeds may surprise you," Bonk says.

The most affectionate breeds include:

- Golden retrievers
- Labradors
- Pomeranians
- Cavalier King Charles Spaniels
- Pugs
- Chihuahuas
- Newfoundland's
- Maltese
- Shih Tzu's

Even if the huge dogs on this list can't curl up on your lap, Bernal says that larger dogs "view their size as no obstacle to getting in close." So, clear some space on the couch. Bernal also points out that mixed breed rescue dogs can be just as cuddly as any other dog. It's not entirely due to the breed (yes, grumpy golden retrievers exist).

There are always exceptions to the norm, so "select the best dog for your family" by considering the individual dog, overall breed features, as well as your family's lifestyle.

The Human Element

The analysts didn't pardon human personality characteristics from having some impact, regardless of whether positive or negative. For instance, the study observed a relationship between the degree that the dog progressed during a behavioral intervention/modification and good faith.

The five principles are essential when utilizing the Big Five character model to assess personality. Numerous mental and social scientists use this model to focus on character traits, and it is particularly helpful for studies like this one. We assess a few character types inside our hypothetical structure that relate to scruples. For instance, good behavior and appropriate conduct is frequently esteemed by those who score high on having the Judging characteristic.

The dogs of individuals having this quality were less inclined to show progress in changing forceful conduct toward outsiders, even with training and efforts at behavioral modification. The scientists believe that the scrupulous animal people's way of life and practices had molded their dogs in such a way that they show more regional animosity toward others.

The analysts also observed that the dogs of extraverted animal owners were more likely to succeed at diminishing nonsocial feelings of trepidation (apprehension about thunder or other boisterous commotions, for instance) and contact awareness within 90 days of social intercession. Interestingly, introverts tend to form a more meaningful connection with their dogs, or as the study says, they might show "more protection from disconnecting themselves" from their pets. Nonetheless, the study expresses that other research has shown that extroverts will generally report more close-knit connections with their dogs than introverts.

Transparency, another Big Five characteristic, is a quality that a portion of our sixteen character types have shown. It most frequently arises a statement of the Intuitive attribute. Dogs living with owners who exhibit transparency showed a diminishing apprehension about exposure to new dogs over time. The scientists hypothesized that more open individuals are likely to rely on more current and up-to-date procedures and socialization efforts in training their dogs.

Of course, this study does not shape or form the final word on pets and character. "Further examination is required," was a consistent refrain throughout the study. Yet, there could be something there, and it is certainly interesting for those pet people who have a background in psychology or an interest in personality profiles. There will doubtlessly be more studies to come on this and related topics, so stay tuned.

CATS AND OWNERS SHARE SIMILAR PERSONALITY TRAITS

Cats are frequently stereotyped as being substantially less amiable than dogs. While it is true that they will generally be considerably more autonomous than dogs, another study was undertaken to determine whether there may be something else involved in constructing a cat's character besides genetics. A group from the University of Helsinki says they've recognized seven unmistakable characteristics and conduct attributes that cats show consistently.

Cats are one of our most common and well-known pets. However, for the sheer number of them we welcome into our homes, surprisingly little is known about their behavior compared to dogs. However, feline behavior is progressively being explored. A particular focus of many of these studies is that of cat characteristics and how they develop, which determined that cat owners should anticipate that the expected characteristics may vary based on the feline variety they bring into their homes. Utilizing a far-reaching survey of cat owners, scientists analyzed the behavior and character tendencies of more than 4,300 cats across 26 distinct varieties.

Cats truly become beloved members of our families, even to the point that they take on human propensities—both positive and negative—and adjust their way of life to fit that of their owners. The research shows how significantly bonding and affection can influence specific animals. While hereditary qualities certainly help to mold some parts of character and conduct, a singular cat's current circumstances are a critical component to its overall personality as well.

What's on a Cat's Mind?

Professor Hannes Lohi of the University of Helsinki had a team study cat personality and behavior by asking a group of cat owners a series of 138 questions. The authors of the study identified seven distinct traits and tendencies of cats based on the responses:

Activity/Playfulness

- Fearfulness
- Aggression towards humans
- Sociability towards humans
- Sociability towards cats
- Litter box issues (relieving themselves in inappropriate places or displaying poor litter box cleanliness)
- Excessive grooming

Not all cats are alike. Along with discovering the various personalities that our furry friends may exhibit, the team has noted that some breeds exhibit more of one specific attribute than others. It turns out that terms like "frisky cats" and "scaredy cats" are more than just a saying.

The scientists indicated that "The Russian Blue was the most frightened breed, while the Abyssinian was the least. The Bengal breed was the most active, while the Persian and other Exotic breeds were the least active. The Siamese and Balinese breeds exhibited the most obsessive grooming, while the Turkish Van rated significantly higher in hostility against humans and lower in sociability toward cats. In a previous investigation, we had seen the same phenomenon."

The findings found several intriguing connections between the personality of the cat owner and the character, lifestyle, and well-being of the cat:

1. **Openness.** More open cat owners...
- Had friendlier cats.
- Had less aggressive cats.
- Had less aloof cats.
- Were less likely to allow their cat to roam outside freely (an unexpected finding).
- Had more cats.

2. **Conscientiousness.** More conscientious cat owners...
- Had friendlier cats.
- Had less aggressive cats.
- Had less aloof cats.
- Had less anxious/fearful cats.
- Had more cats.

3. **Extroversion.** More extroverted cat owners...
- Had friendlier cats.
- Were more likely to have a cat of normal weight.

- Were more likely to allow their cat to roam outside freely.
- Had fewer cats.

4. **Agreeableness.** More agreeable cat owners...
- Had less aggressive cats.
- Had less aloof cats.
- Were more likely to have a cat of normal weight.
- Had fewer cats.
- Were happier with their cats.

5. **Neuroticism.** More neurotic cat owners...
- Had more aggressive cats.
- Had more anxious/fearful cats.
- Were more likely to have a cat with a "behavioral problem."
- Were more likely to have a cat with a medical problem.
- Were more likely to have a cat with a stress-related illness
- Were more likely to have an overweight cat.
- Were more likely to own a non-pedigree (mixed breed) cat.
- Were less likely to allow their cat to roam outside freely.
- Had fewer cats.

Also, family cats were viewed as more amiable, less forceful, less standoffish, and less restless than non-family (arbitrarily reared) cats. They were additionally bound to be kept inside and more averse to be permitted to wander outside unrestrained.

In general, as expected, a cat owner's neuroticism resulted in poor wellbeing and conduct results in a cat. At the same time, the other character qualities (receptiveness, uprightness, extraversion, and pleasantness) led to much more positive results. The scientists believed that masochistic cat owners might be overprotective, dictatorial, or capricious. Researchers were unable to formulate a hypothesis for why hypochondriacs were more bound to claim a non-family cat but suggest that these individuals might have noticed a character match in their cat. Perhaps these people favor cats that are more forceful, restless, and detached (qualities more normal in non-family cats).

Past research shows that cat owners are the most joyful with their cats when they coordinate well regarding showing warmth and closeness. Strangely, cat owners were likewise most joyful when their cats varied from them in terms of strength/accommodation. Research on dogs has not observed a connection between the owner's neuroticism and dog variety; nonetheless, owners high in the attribute of "psychoticism" are more likely to claim a dog variety generalized as forceful.

The study additionally divulged fascinating outcomes concerning indoor versus cats with access to open-air environments. Cats that were not permitted to wander outside freely showed more pressure-related sickness. It is conceivable that owners of indoor cats were better able to recognize and report such sickness. Yet, as indicated by the researchers, this is improbable as indoor and open-air cats didn't vary in their non-stress-related wellbeing results. Discoveries about cats kept indoors versus those allowed open-air access should be deciphered cautiously, as most members lived in the UK, where the standard is to permit a cat to roam outside (just 26% were indoor-only cats). The pressure that a cat encounters inside versus outside may likewise rely vigorously upon the specific open-air climate (e.g., whether it is metropolitan, rural, or rustic).

Parrot

HORSES AND OWNERS SHARE SIMILAR PERSONALITY TRAITS

Most equestrians are well aware that there are numerous interesting horse personality traits and characteristics. Similar to individuals, these attributes shape their conduct and how they handle different circumstances. It can require some investment of time for your horse's actual character to sparkle; however, remain patient! Their peculiarities and unique and highly individual attributes will become undeniable on their schedule. You will wonder how you didn't see them there in the first place!

In the equine world, certain predominant horse character types surface repeatedly. Your horse might be categorized as one of these classes or a blend of several. When you recognize your horse's character characteristics, it will be easier to train them. Your connection and communication with each other can improve dramatically!

A powerful connection can be thought of as a link with a person or thing that triggers you to experience a scope of sentiments, even without any direct contact. Horses and people might foster this deep connection or trust and affection through communication, riding, or training and daily care.

Specific horses might give indications of acknowledgment when you or different people approach them. Suppose there are other horses nearby and an owner chooses to embrace another horse. In that case, the original horse might give signals that are indications of ownership or desire, as another horse has moved in on their property. However, this doesn't imply that the horse's actions are always genuinely connected to its owner. Instead, it may simply be responding to one more animal in what they see as their domain or living space.

How we communicate with our horses is critical to connecting with them. Always take note that how we approach them and converse with them can support specific goals, if nothing else. Moving toward a horse forcefully while yelling orders will yield adverse outcomes than, for example, placing a firm but gentle hand on their flank and addressing them more calmly. A horse will figure out how to pay attention to what you are saying, thereby comprehending and responding to your fundamental prompts and orders more readily. The horse will learn how to trust you, which may, in turn, allow the horse to shape a bond with you.

Understanding our feelings and how we respond to specific emotions might assist us with understanding horses' reactions and goals. We might react anxiously to fear or excitedly to seeing our friends and family after long periods. You might notice that the horse will respond with concern when exposed to a situation that makes it fearful, and likewise, the horse may dash over to see you once they remember you.

There is proof enough, through extensive research, to cause us to believe that there is a relationship between a dog's enthusiastic associations with its owner and being taken care of and focused on. How can we determine if this is the case with horses? One can assume that if they know when to expect their food consistently, subsequently, this might be something they react to with love. It's reasonable to assume that they wouldn't react negatively to somebody who cares for them.

Dogs themselves might vary in their responses and reactions from that of horses. Dogs have been known to stand by and pine at entryways, trusting that their owners will return. You might see that they respond tragically or forcefully when another person or different animals attempt to stand out enough to be noticed by their owner. There is even proof to suggest that dogs can detect their owner's troubles and even smell low glucose in people. They might attempt to remain around you and 'request' to be embraced or try to sit with you, which are obvious indicators of a bond. Dogs have likewise been known to 'grieve' the loss of their owners when they pass on by showing unmistakable indications of misery and misfortune. For example, some dogs have remained near their owner's grave or place of death crying and refusing to eat.

Considering all of this, it's reasonable to assume that there is a type of deep bond or passionate connection between dogs and their owners. There are many similarities between the actions of dogs and horses, which might show that horses do form similar types of connections. However, a few important contrasts between the two species should be noted.

Some dog breeds were created as 'working' dogs. They are urged to act in specific ways to accomplish a task and depend on human prompts and support to do the work. A deeper connection may form between the dog and that individual based on shared goals and the rewards of working together.

Comparatively, horses typically have a herd mentality, where they like to mingle with others of the same species and incline toward one another for solace and assurance. When horses are kept, most training techniques are utilized to show the horse that the human is the herd chief. This results in a cozy relationship with the human once the horse figures out that trusting the human is essential for the stability of the herd.

Additionally, we take our dogs for walks which provides the opportunity to exercise for both the human and the dog and allows for a valuable connection and trust to be fostered. We communicate with horses in comparative ways. If we are going to train a horse to be ridden and interacted with, we must first get them to trust us. Working with a horse to get to the point of riding gives the horse and human a shared goal—like with the working dog—that can perhaps lead to a deeper connection.

In certain regards, the horse looks to us for approval and prompts as they may do with their herd chief. This can demonstrate trust, yet additionally, it illustrates the presence of a working relationship as it is the advantage that the human gets from the riding that is the fundamental distinction between connections

Indisputably, people can bond with their horses and dogs on various levels and in multiple ways. Dogs plainly show fear of abandonment, often from one specific owner, and exhibit possessive characteristics. While they genuinely perceive and develop a unique relationship with their owners, horses have a significantly more herd-like mindset concerning their connections.

Common Horse Personalities

Challenging

The difficult horse will push you to your limits. They are not just the herd's leader, but they may also attempt to lead you! Gaining their respect can be difficult. You have a possibility of effectively riding this horse if you use clear and well-timed aids. However, you must be conscious of every indicator. With them, there's no slacking!

Fearful

A terrified horse is usually referred to as a spooked horse. They can become anxious in new places or situations. They have a strong desire to flee. An experienced and patient person is required to gain trust from these horses. Riders and handlers should always be alert of their surroundings since they react quickly. Don't be caught off guard by this type of horse.

Grumpy

Is your horse pinning its ears all the time? You may have got a grump on your hands. This horse may be uninterested in humans, the barn, and even other horses. Everything appears to make them unhappy! These horses are frequently seen with pinned ears, a swishing tail, and bared fangs. Grumpy horses have no qualms about biting or kicking! You'll need quick reflexes.

Sensitive

A sensitive horse is seen as a prize by certain riders. This type of horse can be dangerous in the wrong hands. A sensitive horse is usually forward in the saddle, responds to aid lightly, and works hard. They are, on the other hand, ready to take offense. If these horses don't understand the aid appropriately, they may become panicked or flee. They perform best when ridden by a skilled rider.

Easy-Going

The easy-going horse is gentle and understanding, making it ideal for new riders. They won't become enraged if the aids aren't correct. They're quite forgiving! Their calm demeanor enables them to deal with new events with ease. They are, however, a bit on the sluggish side. The laid-back horse may lack the strut necessary to place in the winner's circle in shows. They will, nevertheless, instill great confidence in you!

Social

These horses infringe upon everyone's business. They're the ones who dangle their heads over the stall doors, demanding to be scratched or patted! Having a horse interested in its surroundings can be a wonderful thing. They're obedient and relatively simple to train. On the other hand, these horses have shorter attention spans and can be demanding. They insist on being in your personal space, which is disrespectful. A firm handler is frequently required!

Pleaser

This group is gold to equestrians because they are loyal and diligent. Their characteristics are comparable to those of sensitive people. This horse tends to be forward, on the aids, and quick to react. It's not necessary to tell them things twice. While they have an incredible work ethic, they can become impatient with an inexperienced rider. Aids must be sharp and understandable because they are so eager to please.

Most horses fall into several groups, but one typically stands out above the rest. Depending on your needs, some personality features may be more appealing to you. An easy-going horse is best for novice or hesitant riders, whereas competent riders prefer a sensitive type.

Horse Characteristics: Physical, Behavior, And Fun Facts
It's intriguing to learn that all horses have similar qualities, even though they are raised differently and used for different purposes. Horses are unique individuals, yet some physical and behavioral features are universal.

Horses have a variety of physical qualities that distinguish them from other animals, including large hooves, large eyes, and a small stomach. Horses also have particular habits, such as grazing all day and bolting when they detect danger. Horses have several remarkable features, including the inability to vomit (even if they want to) and the ability to sleep standing up.

Understanding the personality features and qualities of a horse can aid in the development of a successful relationship with it. This understanding is also helpful during training since it allows you to understand how your horse thinks, making the process go more smoothly.

Here are some of the most important characteristics of horses:

Unique Horse Characteristics

1. **Prey Animals**
Horses are prey animals; thus, they are constantly on the lookout for danger. Most horses are readily spooked by things that people might not consider dangerous.

As a rider, it's critical to teach your horse not to be afraid and desensitize it to noises so that it doesn't startle anytime something loud occurs nearby, which could cause it to bolt before you even realize what's going on.

2. **Alert**

Your horse is continually on the lookout for danger, is sensitive to its environment, and is aware of its surroundings at all times. This is why your 'buddy' will be directing its ears in various directions at any given time, hoping to pick up a sound you may have missed.

Horses communicate over vast distances using these ear placements and subtle motions like swishing tails. You may be familiar with the term "horse sense." It refers to the horse's acute awareness of the threats that surround it. It's what keeps a horse safe and enables it to avoid danger.

3. **Creatures of Habit**

Feeding, grooming, and training your horse consistently each morning are excellent habits to develop. Horses are animals of habit, anticipating occurrences throughout the day, which is why they tend to be healthier and perform better when on stable timetables.

4. **Herd Animals**

Horses are herd animals who rely0 on one another for safety and friendship. There is a "pecking order" in any herd, and each horse has a defined function or obligation. These responsibilities keep the members safe and organized.

While the main stallion and mare keep an eye out for predators like wolves, mountain lions, and coyotes, other horses have responsibilities such as being sentinels, tending to newborns, and grazing, so they don't all have to eat at the same time—they work together!

5. **Sensitive Animals**

Horses are highly sensitive and emotional animals who can create deep emotional relationships with people. Most horses prefer being with others, whether they're grazing in a herd or enjoying the friendship of a human companion.

6. **Herbivores**

Horses are herbivores, meaning they eat forage (grass and hay) to stay strong and meet their nutritional requirements. On the other hand, hard-working horses may require a grain-supplemented diet to provide them with extra energy.

Three Behavior Traits Horses Display

Understanding horse behavior can help us better care for our animals by ensuring that we feed them correctly and provide them with appropriate exercise.

1. **Horses graze most of the day.**

Horses have been around for approximately 25 million years. They have evolved to live in areas with low-quality food by grazing for most of the day. Horses advanced this mind-blowing capacity to concentrate and utilize supplements from low-level rummages while living on the fields of the Eurasian Steppe.

It isn't out of lethargy that your horse grazes the entire day but instead need. Horses' method of eating includes slow, consistent digestion. Eating and moving fill two needs: digestion of food and exercise.

Horses restricted in stalls need "turn out time" with the goal that they stay solid and healthy! Horses are ordinarily open-minded toward temperature changes, and in the fields, they can encounter outrageous variances.

Horses adjust to these temperatures very well; nonetheless, their needs can change based on factors like age, activity level, and general wellbeing. More youthful horses probably won't require any blanketing around evening or when it is cold outside, while more seasoned ones will need a horse cover to keep warm when temperatures drop.

2. **Horses communicate through body language.**

Horses have their own language, and humans must understand it to train them effectively. Their "speech" includes neighing, head placement, pinning ears when agitated, and other forms of nonverbal communication and body movement. Horses communicate with one another just as humans do. They are social animals who have a deep knowledge of each other's feelings.

3. **Horses need to move around.**

Some of a horse's organs must move for them to operate correctly. They spend practically all of their waking hours outdoors, either looking for food, grazing, or walking to a water source. Horses must walk for various purposes, including to wear down their hooves and keep their blood flowing. The hoof functions as a pump to return blood to the horse's heart.

To keep your horse healthy, you should house him in a way that allows him to move around as much as possible. If your horse is kept in a stall, you must let it out every day to ensure it can exercise and move around.

Human Characteristics of Horses

Believe it or not, your horse may be more human than you think! Horses exhibit four human characteristics.

Here are some similarities between horses and humans:

1. **Horses can read human emotions.**

A horse has an uncanny ability to read its human handler. It can determine when a rider is dissatisfied or scared right away.

Buck Brannaman has a phrase that brilliantly summarizes this: "The Horse is a reflection of your soul, and what you see in the mirror may not always be flattering."

This means that a horse can reflect your feelings and, on occasion, may even reveal aspects of your personality that you are unaware of.

2. **Horses and humans are pretty similar physically.**

Horses and humans sharing comparable physical qualities may seem absurd, but they have several shared physical attributes. While horses have a larger bone structure, humans and horses have a similar number of bones: a horse has 205 bones, while humans have 206. Although both animals have a single stomach and pelvis, horses' stomachs can digest cellulose fiber from the grass they consume, whereas humans' stomachs cannot.

3. Horses are smart.

Horses are intelligent, and they may be trained to perform a variety of athletics and performances.

4. Horses have good memories.

Like most humans, horses have excellent memories. They forgive, but they won't forget!

The Characteristics Associated with Horses According to the Chinese Zodiac

Each year is connected with an animal in Chinese culture, which symbolizes the qualities of persons born in that year. People born in the Year of the Horse are believed to be bright, independent, successful, and ambitious—all qualities that, if embraced, can help you achieve your goals.

What are the Mean Horse Breeds?

Horses typically become hostile or harsh only when humans or other animals mistreat them because their basic tendency is to avoid confrontation rather than fight. When confronted, however, hot-blooded horse breeds like Thoroughbreds, Arabians, Akhal-Tekes, and Barbs are the first to fight back.

DO PETS TAKE ON THEIR OWNER'S PERSONALITY?

Your pet doesn't share your hereditary qualities, yet on the off chance that you chose your pet, it's conceivable your dog or cat is significantly like you.

Are you and your pet the same? This is one of those nature versus nurture questions with a twist. Your pet doesn't share your hereditary qualities. However, assuming you chose your pet (rather than gaining him through some arbitrary situation), it's conceivable you—either intentionally or subliminally—chose a dog or cat that is very much like you in temperament and personality. It's additionally possible that, regardless of how you obtained your pet, the two of you have become more similar as you have shared your lives. Regardless of how you got your pet, you more than likely share more than a few character attributes.

Take the instance of Midnight, a mixed breed dog who gave off an impression of being the laziest of the litter. He rested as his littermates played. The mother and two youngsters who adopted him had very different personality characteristics. At some point, the dog took on the shaggy looks and solid character of one of the children. Perhaps it was because they connected as good friends, or maybe because the child was frequently upset, and the dog detected that he required him most. Both Midnight and his male owner were insightful, rebellious, and daring. Both would seek out adventures. Also, both appeared to have a guardian angel on their backs, as they each endured mishaps that put their lives in significant danger and came out alright.

Cats Use Personality Traits to Get What They Want

Now, for a story about cats. Magritte and Cassatt were two dark-striped cats who were indistinguishable when they were adopted as family pets. Both were active and perky. However, as they developed, Cassatt took on the aggregate personality characteristics of the three youngsters in the house. It is assumed that she had concluded that to stand out enough to be noticed, she should become exactly like them—and even act as a rival. However, she was incredibly tender and sweet with their mother. Magritte observed this shocking conduct from a distance. Whenever a youngster crept in bed with Mom, Cassatt demanded attention by pressing between the mother and her child. This cat additionally figured out how to make her whimpers sound like "Mother," which was somewhat unnerving.

When the cats visited Grandma, Magritte seemed to see his opening. He was the more socially developed cat at any rate. However, in this new climate and surroundings, the cat assumed the character attributes of his new companion. Without the constant interruption of the kids, he could sparkle as the tranquil, insightful cat. This cat charmed himself to Grandma by acting very much like her. He would sit at her PC as though he were working, go through her record cabinet as though searching for a document, and sit by her books, staring at them as though attempting to understand them. Whatever

Grandma did, he needed to do too. In any case, the cat's endeavor to access a glass of iced tea did not go well and led to a major mess. Grandma wasn't quite charmed after that little stunt—but forgiveness is also essential when you have pets!

What do Scientists Say About Pet Personality Traits?

At least two researchers we are aware of have explored owner and pet characteristics in connection with one another. Professor Richard Wiseman of the University of Hertfordshire led a web-based overview of animal people and observed that dog and cat owners shared such character attributes as satisfaction, knowledge, autonomy, and awareness of what's funny with their pets.

Dr. Sam Gosling, who coordinates the Human and Animal Personality Lab at the University of Texas, applied analytical human character testing on dogs. He had previously accepted the idea that the personality characteristics of animals were only what individual humans projected onto them. However, he found that particular qualities could very precisely be distinguished in dogs. He expects that his exploration can be utilized to more appropriately coordinate shelter and rescue dogs with the most appropriately suited owners. It could also assist individuals with choosing the best dogs to perform explicit obligations of working dogs, such as police work or aiding the disabled.

You and your cat or dog are most likely more indistinguishable than you're even mindful of at the personality level. Be that as it may, ask somebody who knows both you and your pet very well whether they notice your common character qualities. You and your pet may be just like twins without you even knowing it!

WHY WE RELY ON ANIMALS FOR HEALING

Having a pet can dramatically increase the quality of your life. Scientific studies indicate that people who own pets gain some unique benefits. Your pet can boost your emotional, mental, and physical health. Pets generally increase the bliss that we experience in life. Here are the reasons why having a pet will make you a better and happier person.

1. You become more responsible.
When you take on ownership of a pet, you effectively accept the burden of caring for another animal's life. You must feed, water, clean up after, and maintain your pet's health, as well as provide it with adequate activity. This will motivate you to be more responsible at work, with your family, and in other areas of your life. You become a better person as a result of this new commitment.

2. Pets can make you bond more closely with the community
Pets are well-known for their ability to break the ice. People are more likely to stop and say hello to you when you're walking your dog or playing with your cat outside. Neighbors and

passers-by will notice your pet's cuteness. They're also inclined to tell you about their dogs, which often leads to a satisfying chat. As a result, pets can help you learn more about your neighbors and improve your social life.

3. **You can handle pressure and the challenges of life in a better way.**

Did you know that your pet can provide you with hope while you're going through a difficult moment in your life? Making a positive difference in the lives of others while facing your problems, according to psychologists, is therapeutic. Caring for your pet can help you feel better while going through your own life challenges and daily struggles, which enables you to develop emotional strength and makes you a better person over time.

4. **Pets make you more active.**

You can engage in a variety of daily activities with your pet. Tossing a ball in the park with your dog or dancing around with your cat are just a few examples. These activities are beneficial to your cardiovascular health and provide healthy exercise. Furthermore, they elevate your mood and increase your energy levels. Statistics show that people who own dogs walk for seventy-nine percent longer than those who do not.

5. **You increase your communication skills.**

Your pet is unable to communicate with you verbally. As a result, you'll have to converse with it through nonverbal means, such as gestures or touch. This helps you to improve your nonverbal communication skills. It also aids in your development as a patient listener.

6. Pets can relax you and make you calm.

Our furry companions may help us become peaceful, relaxed, and stress-free, which is a fantastic fact. Studies have shown that having a pet can help you maintain a stable heart rate in stressful situations, helping you relax and become a happier person.

7. Getting a pet helps you to love yourself more.

Pets can foster self-love and increase self-esteem, according to psychologists worldwide. Do you have a minor case of depression? Get a pet and learn to love unconditionally. Pet owners are far less lonely. As a result, they are happier and more appreciative of their dogs and themselves.

8. Pets are natural mood boosters.

Did you realize that playing with your pet might make you happier? Dopamine is a neurotransmitter that exists in all of our brains. It is linked to pleasure and reward. This hormone is released, and its levels in your body rise when you play with your pet.

9. Pets help you to become more affectionate.

The activities you undergo while engaging with and caring for your pet can make you more affectionate in the long run. Cleaning and playing with your pet are genuine shows of love and care. You may find yourself extending this expression to your human counterparts as you perform them daily. You will become a more affectionate and better person as a result of this.

10. You become more empathetic by having a pet.

People who had pets as children develop into adults who are far more compassionate, according to behavioral psychologists.

Taking care of their pets taught them to nurture and pay attention to others. As a result, individuals continue to use these abilities as adults and have more satisfying relationships. This has the consequence of making them happy people.

11. **Your pet can make you laugh more.**

Pet owners agree that our furry buddies can be rather amusing. Dogs and cats are capable of making us laugh in a variety of ways. According to psychologists, laughter is highly therapeutic, and it can reduce stress levels. As a result, we are happier.

12. **Having a pet can make you live longer.**

Did you know that owning a pet boosts your chances of living a long and healthy life? Having a pet can prevent life-threatening conditions, including high blood pressure and heart disease. This successfully extends and improves your life.

13. **Pets help eliminate loneliness.**

You can be lonely for a variety of reasons. Bereavement, children moving out, and divorce are all examples of ways loneliness can develop. If you find yourself in one of these situations, owning a pet can help you feel less lonely. A pet will provide you with affection and company. You will feel less lonely and happy as a result of this.

14. **You learn how to invest your emotions more efficiently.**

Having a pet necessitates emotional investment in your interactions. You must look after your pet's health, love them, and even defend them. Each of these actions represents an emotional expression. You learn to regulate your emotions more efficiently in other aspects of your life by expressing yourself in these ways. You grow into a more tolerant and better person.

15. **Pets can give you a sense of purpose.**

Pets can help you find a sense of purpose in your life by making you feel wanted and needed. The knowledge that your pet relies on you gives you a sense of self-worth. Having a pet provides you with a daily routine that you strive to maintain. As a result, you have a reason to get out of bed every day. It adds meaning, purpose, and happiness to your existence.

16. **You become more sociable by having a pet.**

People who have dogs have a better social life, according to studies. On the street or the bus, they are more inclined to strike up a discussion with strangers because dogs strengthen your social skills and increase your self-esteem. As a result, you will improve as a person.

17. **Pets promote discipline in our lives.**

Once you get a pet, you must establish a routine for caring for it. You set aside time for activities such as playing, eating, bathing, and relaxing. You can improve your capacity to stay disciplined by setting and keeping to a daily plan. This makes it easier for you to cope in other aspects of your life, such as balancing your employment or career tasks and offers you a sense of fulfillment and contentment.

18. **You develop emotional and mental flexibility.**

Pets are known to do various unexpected things that you will have to learn to deal with. They can wake up from their snooze and poop in an inconvenient location. They can also jump into your guest's lap and scare them. Understanding and responding to this behavior appropriately is an integral part of owning a pet. You will grow more mentally and emotionally flexible as a result of this. You become a better person as a result of this.

19. **Keeping a pet makes you more attractive.**

Having a pet increases your attractiveness to those around you. You appear more kind, trustworthy, and approachable if you have a pet. According to studies, persons accompanied by a pet are more inclined to chat with strangers than those who do not. Your pet helps you live a happy life by making you more attractive.

20. **You become more forgiving.**

There are many things your pet can do to irritate you. They are capable of chewing on your prized shoes, breaking your cherished vase, and peeing on your carpets. You simply have to understand and forgive them when they do this. This tendency to forgive extends to your interpersonal relationships with others. You have a natural ability to forgive and retain inner serenity. As a result, you improve as a person.

The Important Take Away

We have had pets in our homes for ages. They offer a variety of benefits to our lives. A few of them have already been mentioned, but your pets may provide additional comforts, and they are reasons to love our animals even more. If you don't already have a pet, you should consider whether a pet is right for you, so you may also experience these advantages!

THERAPEUTIC EFFECT OF ANIMALS AS PETS

People dealing with various health issues can benefit from animal-assisted therapy to relieve pain and anxiety. Pet therapy is growing in popularity in the medical field and beyond. Discover the origins of this burgeoning trend.

What Is Pet Therapy?

Pet therapy refers to animal-assisted therapy as well as other animal-assisted activities. Animal-assisted therapy is a rapidly expanding discipline that employs dogs or other animals to assist people in recovering from or coping with health issues such as heart disease, cancer, and mental health disorders. On the other hand, animal-assisted activities serve a broader goal, such as bringing comfort and entertainment to nursing home residents.

How Does Animal-Assisted Therapy Work?

Assume you're a patient in a hospital. Your doctor asks if you'd be interested in the hospital's animal-assisted therapy program. You say yes, and your doctor arranges for someone to explain the program to you in greater detail. You learn that an assistance dog and its handler will visit your hospital room and stay for around ten or fifteen minutes. You are welcome to pet the dog and ask questions of the handler during this first meeting.

Who Can Benefit from Animal-Assisted Therapy?

Animal-assisted therapy can considerably relieve pain, anxiety, sadness, and fatigue in persons with various health issues. Some examples of people that can be helped by animal-assisted therapy include:

- Children undergoing dental procedures
- People receiving cancer treatment
- People in long-term care facilities
- People with cardiovascular diseases
- People with dementia
- Veterans with post-traumatic stress disorder
- People with anxiety
- Stroke victims and people undergoing physical therapy to regain motor skills

However, people facing health difficulties aren't the only ones who benefit. Animal visitors' family members and friends say they feel better as well.

Pet therapy is also being employed in non-medical contexts to assist individuals in coping with anxiety and stress, such as at universities and community activities.

Does Pet Therapy Have Risks?
Safety and sanitation are the most pressing concerns related to pet therapy, particularly in hospital settings. The animals permitted to participate in these programs must be hygienic, vaccinated, well-trained, and checked for appropriate behavior and temperament to access hospitals and other facilities that offer pet therapy.

Back to our example… You discover you're smiling after the visit with the dog and handler. And you're a little less fatigued and more upbeat as a result. You can't wait to tell your friends and family about that adorable dog. You're looking forward to the next visit from the dog.

What are the Benefits of Pet Therapy?
Pet therapy takes on the human-animal bond that already exists, heightens it, and applies a new focus. As discussed previously, many physical and mental difficulties can be alleviated by interacting with a friendly pet.

Pet therapy can be employed in a variety of settings. Your progress will be recorded and tracked during organized sessions, and your defined objectives will be an essential component of therapy.

Humans may feel less anxious when a pet is present during medical treatment. When engaging with a pet during rehabilitation, people may be more motivated to recover and perform their therapy. People with sensory impairments may find it easier to communicate with animals than humans. More engagement with healthcare practitioners and other individuals may be encouraged due to this.

What are the Risks of Pet Therapy?

Safety and cleanliness are two of the most significant dangers associated with pet therapy. Pet therapy may cause adverse responses in people who are allergic to animal dander. Pet therapy animals are frequently evaluated for temperament and health to ensure the safety of those interacting with them. Additionally, to help ensure a good experience, an animal's owner and handler must also undergo training and evaluation.

Adverse human impacts are rare in pet therapy, although bites or other unexpected occurrences can happen when unsuitable animals are utilized or if the animals are treated incorrectly. Another risk of pet therapy is that people undergoing treatment may become attached to the animals assisting them and be hesitant to give them up after a session. Low self-esteem and a period of sadness might arise due to this.

How is Pet Therapy Administered?

Pet therapy will be administered by your doctor or the therapist in charge of your treatment. A qualified handler, usually the pet's owner, will accompany the animal to each visit and work closely with your doctor or therapist to help you achieve your objectives. In the majority of situations, the handlers are volunteers. A discussion on proper pet handling is required to protect the safety of both the person receiving therapy and the pet.

The selection of a suitable animal is the first stage in pet therapy. Many organizations provide training and connect volunteer pet owners and caregivers with healthcare experts. A team must meet certain conditions before an animal and its handler can engage in pet therapy. This procedure usually entails the following:

- An examination of the animal to ensure that it is up-to-date on vaccinations and disease-free.
- Lessons in animal obedience to enable complete animal control at all times
- A training course that teaches the handler how to communicate effectively with others
- Discussions with the handler about the animal's disposition, temperament, and characteristics that will make it a promising therapy pet

- Certification through the sponsoring organization

Animals are assigned for therapy depending on a specific person's needs once an animal and a handler team have been approved. The type, breed, size, age, and natural temperament of the animal will decide where and how it will be most helpful.

Outlook

Setting realistic goals and expectations is critical to the effectiveness of pet therapy. These objectives will be determined by each patient and their doctor or therapist at the start of treatment. You'll also talk about how you'll get there and how long it'll take. The doctor or therapist will keep track of your progress and assist you in sticking to your goals. They may alter your treatment plan if your improvement is slower or faster than expected.

Both children and adults can benefit from pet therapy for many physical and mental conditions. It can help alleviate stress, anxiety, and sadness while boosting happiness and socialization. Consult your doctor for further information on pet therapy to see whether it is right for you.

Dog

THERAPY DOGS

People are learning more and more about the health benefits of dogs these days. As a result, there has been a surge in public interest in therapy dogs. Therapy dogs provide solace to those who are anxious, comfort the grieving or lonely, and offer affection to humans in institutions such as hospitals, nursing homes, and schools. If you have a friendly, well-behaved dog who enjoys being around people, you and other dog owners may be asking how therapy dogs are trained.

What is a Therapy Dog?

A therapy dog provides comfort and affection to those in a facility setting or who may benefit from pet visits to deal with a physical or emotional problem. Therapy dogs are not service dogs, which perform a specific service for a person with a disability and are allowed full access to the public under the Americans with Disabilities Act (ADA). They're also not emotional support animals, which require a prescription from a mental health or health care practitioner but don't require any specific training or certification to perform their duties.

Why Train a Therapy Dog?

Therapy dogs provide numerous physical advantages to the people they visit. They may aid in reducing blood pressure and heart rate while elevating endorphins and oxytocin levels in patients. It is not, however, a one-way street. Therapy dogs have been demonstrated to benefit from their work in studies. Therapy dogs exhibit higher levels of endorphins and oxytocin than normal family pets.

"Therapy dogs visit hospitals, nursing homes, libraries, schools, and sites of natural disasters. Linda Keehn, CPDT-KA, therapy dog trainer, evaluator, handler, and owner of Positive Dog Training and Services in New York, says, "Basically any place where there is a need and it would be useful for the dogs to be there."

You can't, for example, take your dog to see a relative in the hospital. Therapy dogs must be certified by a respected national organization then registered with them. However, certification is only the final step in the long journey to becoming a therapy dog, which involves temperament testing, training, and more.

Can Any Dog Be a Therapy Dog?
Even though your dogs might give you unlimited love and affection, that doesn't automatically qualify them as a solid match for treatment work. Similarly, just because you may be a sympathetic individual, you may not be an ideal addition to a dog therapy treatment group. So, what makes a decent treatment dog? And how can handlers become effective dog therapy providers?

Treatment dogs have likely already reached adulthood, with numerous associations not permitting dogs under a year old. Also, many associations expect dogs to pass the AKC Canine Good Citizen (CGC) test for obedience and behavior, while others require a treatment-focused test instead of the CGC.

Keehn, who trains and assesses dogs for CGC and treatment accreditation, certifies that the components included on these tests are critical for when any treatment dog is out in the open. A dog who can't "leave it" on the sign or agreeably communicate with kids won't succeed in this line of pet work.

Other than that, age and breed don't make any difference. Keehn has trained dogs as little as a four-pound Yorkshire Terrier and as old as 13-year-old Beagle, both of whom finished their CGC without a hitch. To ensure the dogs are not behaving in a specific way for their trainer, Keehn only tests dogs for whom she's assumed no part in preparing. Besides achieving all of the obedience and temperament portions of testing, the most successful dogs should have an ordinarily friendly demeanor, not be excessively youthful or playful, and enjoy and "need" the work.

"Most dogs love occupations," says Keehn. "At home, your dog's occupation may simply be climbing close by you or something different. In any case, most dogs like some sort of work, and this is a magnificent occupation for them to have. It's not reasonable to give a dog a task that it doesn't need."

Could Your Dog Make a Good Therapy Dog?
Keehn suggests watching your dog intently and impartially at first to determine its actual demeanor in as unbiased a way as possible. In particular, she says, think about whether your dog enjoys receiving love from individuals other than you.

"Does the dog truly appreciate associating with new individuals in various situations?" asks Keehn. "Does it search out consideration from individuals and have a quiet attitude? It very well may be the most delightful dog in your front room, yet not somewhere else. Most frequently in a treatment circumstance, individuals simply need a dog that sits close to them and allows them to pet it."

To put it plainly, treatment dog applicants are generally quiet, agreeable, and warm to outsiders. They are also prepared to be submissive to their handlers and effectively versatile and unfazed by novel commotions, unfamiliar circumstances, scents, and previously unseen hardware. Most treatment dog associations necessitate that the therapy dogs they sponsor are solid and well-trained and undergo regular well-being and health check-ups.

Would You Make a Good Therapy Dog Handler?

Preparing a treatment dog can prompt new encounters for both dog and owner. The dog's reality opens up to a broader scope, and as a team, you're assisting your local area. Keehn suggests enlisting in a public or nearby treatment section that holds get-togethers. That way, both you and your dog find new companions with this shared objective. She additionally underlines that treatment dog work is as beneficial for the individual as it is for the dog. In any case, she alerts that while the handler and the dog work together, in some cases, handlers should expect to take on unanticipated roles during the process. With this in mind, the human handler should be able to communicate effectively with people receiving pet therapy.

"Escaping yourself and rewarding the local area can further develop your own psychological and actual wellbeing," says Keehn. "At the point when you're carrying a dog to a veterans' association or emergency clinic, you might be the main non-clinical individual they're seeing. It very well might be the only genuine discussion they've had for quite a long time. Be ready, as the treatment dog overseer, to associate with the customer. It could be useful to take a therapy dog instructional class."

Another word of wisdom for new handlers is to receive coaching or mentoring from another handler who knows how to train a treatment dog. They will be familiar with what can happen during sessions and can provide valuable guidance that you would otherwise learn at some other point later in the process. Preparation is key. Allude to this trustworthy coach for extra foundational development or discuss their experiences. In any event, Keehn says, most treatment dog associations have printed material or sites that you can peruse for additional information.

Furthermore, you can frequently pick where you and your dog work. If your dog loves kids, you may choose to visit schools or libraries. However, assuming you don't adore kids, you may choose to work in home encounters with adults and the elderly primarily.

How Are Therapy Dogs Trained?

Depending on your desire and budget, you can decide to prepare a treatment dog on your own or with help. Keehn, who assists owners with preparing their dogs as one-half of a treatment group, prompts that you search for a conventional association that lists accomplished coaches on their websites.

Relying on private preparation and training may be excessively costly; therefore, Keehn suggests investigating the CGC test for the ten fundamental requirements. Then, use all available resources, such as YouTube or the local library, to read books and watch videos for training guidance and tips for success. Participating in a group Dog Good Citizen class is another great option that may be more affordable than private training. While the ten skills required by the CGC assessment are important to breeze through, this training, particularly when it is done through positive reinforcement and encouraging feedback, is priceless and endures forever. It strengthens the bond between handler and dog and teaches valuable lessons that will come in handy for pet therapy endeavors and the human/pet life together.

"Each time you communicate with your dog, your dog is getting the hang of something," affirms Keehn. "Build up the conduct you need. Keep your models at a level that your dog can deal with. Be clear in your correspondence with non-verbal and verbal signs. You don't have to contact the dog. They figure out how to follow their essential impulses to sit and set somewhere around doing what's agreeable."

What Are the Differences Between Therapy Dogs, Emotional Support Dogs, and Service Dogs?

Therapy dogs perform essential tasks requiring significant training and certification, but they are not service dogs. While both need training to perform their professions, there are a few key distinctions between the two titles.

The Americans with Disabilities Act (ADA) defines (and protects) service dogs as those who are "individually trained to do labor or execute duties for the benefit of an individual with a disability, including a physical, sensory, psychiatric, intellectual, or other mental condition." Each service dog you meet has been taught to fulfill the specific needs of its handler. Their duties may involve pressing buttons, retrieving dropped items, alerting their handler or others to a medical emergency, reminding their handler to take medication, and any other task that, ultimately, assists the handler. Under the ADA, service dogs are also granted specific authorization, allowing them to join their handlers on aircraft, in restaurants, and other places where pets are otherwise not permitted.

Therapy dogs are not afforded the same rights and advantages as service dogs. Therapy dogs are specially trained to comfort and improve the lives of the individuals they come into contact with. They are helpful in a variety of situations. Therapy dogs undergo generalized training and accompany their owners as volunteers to authorized settings such as hospitals, schools, libraries, and assisted living homes, among other places. Although therapy dogs are working dogs who are trained and certified, they do it on a volunteer basis and spend the majority of their lives as pets.

On the other hand, emotional support animals are not required to be trained or certified and are treated as pets rather than working dogs. This isn't to dismiss the value of emotional support animals, which mental health specialists often recommend to provide companionship and help with discomfort, despair, and anxiety.

The Therapy Dog Certification Process

To qualify as a certified therapy dog, a dog must pass a test that evaluates temperament and obedience abilities, the two pillars of effective dog therapy. The certification process varies for each organization.

Some groups may conduct an obedience and temperament test before following you on several trips to observe the animal in action. Some examinations are conducted individually, while others, such as Comfort Caring Dogs, conduct group tests. "We are not asking them to work that entire time," Harantschuk says of CCD's test, which can run anywhere from ninety minutes to two hours. "We keep them with us for a long time so we can get to know them." Because your needs and interests primarily determine the certifying organization you choose, Harantschuk advises that you do as much research as possible before deciding which assessment to use.

According to Katie Whiteley, Operations Lead, the Alliance of Therapy Dogs demands a background check before the certification test. After that, certified volunteers must make therapeutic visits at least once every three months to maintain their certification and therapy dog status. (Due to Covid-19, this rule is temporarily suspended.)

The Benefits of Therapy Dog Certification

After you decide that your dog has the appropriate temperament to become a therapy dog, the next stage is to choose a sponsoring organization, take the assessment, and become certified.

While some groups or facilities may allow you to bring your dog without certification, Harantschuk highly advises against it for your safety and the safety of your dog and the individuals who interact with your dog. Even if you wish to visit a family member in an assisted care home outside of the therapy dog certification process, experts highly advise against it. Volunteer opportunities, insurance coverage, and confirmation of the abilities required to execute the job properly are the three most critical benefits of therapy dog certification. It's crucial to have insurance coverage because mistakes and accidents happen, and liability insurance is required when visiting most facilities where therapy dogs are used.

Furthermore, while some therapy dog handlers know precisely where they want to volunteer—the local library or elder care home where a family member is staying—this is not true of all therapy dog handlers. The majority of certifying organizations will assist handlers in finding organizations that are a good fit for their requirements and interests.

Deep Pressure Therapy: Teach Your Dog to Calm Your Anxiety
Deep Pressure Therapy (DPT) has been shown in studies to benefit those who suffer from anxiety, autism, self-harming behaviors, and stress in general. This form of non-medicated treatment has been shown to shorten the length of the illness and make it more bearable.

DPT works by having the dog apply light pressure to your body, chest, or injured body area (as in self-harming) depending on the dog's size. You can train smaller dogs to sleep straight over your chest or along the front of your body, while larger breeds can be taught to place their heads or feet across your lap or legs, depending on what is most comfortable for you.

Here are the steps to teaching your dog Deep Pressure Therapy:

1. On the Sofa and Paws Up Command
If your dog isn't used to sitting on a sofa, you may need to use goodies to persuade him—or let him know that it is okay—to do so. Showing your dog the reward, then slowly moving it to the back of the sofa while eagerly yelling his name and, "Paws up!" (For example, "Toby, paws up!") is all it takes. Depending

on his aversion, you may need to reward your dog every time he gets closer to you on the sofa.

2. Practice

If you have a smaller dog, the primary goal is for him to have all four paws on the sofa and then go "down." If you don't want or can't handle your dog's weight, the "paws up" order will be given with his front paws or head on the sofa.

Treats should be used to reinforce the "paws up" command until your dog understands what it means. Once you've mastered this, you can practice it without using treats; you want your dog to do it because you require it, not because there's a treat at the end of the session.

3. Paws Off Command

After that, you'll want to teach your dog the command "paws off." "Paws up" is the same as "paws off," but reversed. To practice, use the command "paws off" to get your dog off the couch. Remember to reward him each time he completes the task.

4. Laying/Sitting on Sofa

Preferably, for DPT to work, you need small-to-medium-size dogs to lie upward along your body with paws on your shoulders and their head close to yours. If you have a huge dog, he will put his paws across your legs or rest his head on your lap while you are in a sitting position.

To prepare your dog, utilize the "paws up" order, followed by the "down" command once he is up with all fours or alongside your lap. When your dog achieves this assignment, give him a treat, trailed by the "paws down" order.

You must rehearse this preparation so that your dog learns to do it on order, without a food prize toward the end. If you are working with a bigger dog on the DPT method, he should incline toward your lap for the pressure to be applied appropriately; in any case, when your dog relaxes, he should naturally apply his weight on your lap.

5. Simulated Anxiety Symptom Training

Once your dog has learned the previous strategies, take it a step further by simulating your symptoms in a stressful environment. It will be easier to work on this learning process when you are relaxed and able to reward your dog for obeying the commands if you practice while you are not in an actual emergency.

Tips For Training a Therapy Dog

Training a therapy dog is a challenging endeavor that frequently demands a lot of effort from the dog and the handler, especially if it is your first time. Sometimes, due to their disposition, even the best-trained dogs in the world will never make good therapy dogs. In contrast, with the correct training method (and some luck!), some difficult-to-train dogs may open up and become terrific therapy dogs. Training is the first step in becoming a therapy dog team. Following the steps below is a surefire way to move forward towards accomplishing your goals:

1. Use the Canine Good Citizen Program

A dedicated handler works with therapy dogs. While this is usually the dog's owner, it isn't always the case. For example, you might think your dog would make an excellent therapy dog but don't have the time to devote to it. In this case, your dog can be taken through the training by another handler. If you and your dog wish to be members of the therapy team, you must both go through a rigorous training program.

Participating in the AKC Canine Good Citizen Program is a terrific place to start (CGC). This certification verifies that your dog is well-socialized, friendly, and well-trained. Maintaining CGC certification is, in fact, a requirement for many therapy dog programs.

2. Work on Training and Behavior Proofing

You should also put a great deal of time and effort into improving your dog's training and behavior proofing. Your dog must be able to remain calm and joyful in the presence of loud noises, movement (both human and object), medical equipment of all types, and any other potential distractions. Most importantly, you should be able to obtain and hold your dog's attention at any time and in any situation. You might want to look for a therapy dog training class offered by a qualified, experienced dog trainer.

3. Research Animal-Assisted Therapy Organizations

While preparing your dog to become the ideal treatment dog, you should also begin investigating official animal-assisted treatment associations. Two globally recognized gatherings are Pet Partners and Therapy Dogs International. Numerous urban areas and districts have their own independent treatment programs, so do some investigation into what's accessible around you and what best fits your needs.

Remember that every animal-assisted treatment bunch is somewhat unique. It might take a bit of exploration and trial and error to discover which group is the best fit for yourself as well as your dog. Each gathering has its norms, required courses, and unique testing necessary for a dog and overseer to officially join an enlisted treatment group.

The different gatherings offer diverse treatment programs, some more heavily focused on one treatment area over others. Your decision might be impacted by where you and your dog most want to go. For example, you might favor a gathering that spotlights on nursing homes or one that consistently visits schools. Find your niche, and you are well on your way to helping your dog achieve top-notch therapy dog status.

4. Document Your Dog's Health

For their safety and the safety of the people they will be visiting, therapy dogs must meet specific health requirements. At the very least, your dog should have all of its vaccines up to date, receive regular heartworm and flea preventative measures, and have a clean bill of health as per your veterinarian.

5. Pass the Final Evaluation

To become an approved animal-assisted therapy team, a dog and its handler must complete a final exam or set of evaluations after meeting all of the prerequisites. The procedure might be time-consuming and demanding at times. However, many dedicated handlers and their dogs find that the effort is well worth it in the end.

6. Behavior Problems

Regardless of how much you might trust that your little guy will transform into the perfect treatment dog, not all dogs will manage to do so. Each dog is unique, so don't be baffled if yours doesn't tolerate the preparation necessary to move forward in the endeavor. If your dog isn't enjoying the training, it won't enjoy the work.

Now and then, as a dog prepares to become a therapy dog, it's discovered that it simply doesn't have the proper disposition or capacity to focus effectively enough to take on the gig. In addition, it is perfectly normal to observe dogs who might not want to invest that much of their energy with outsiders or who become more easily frightened in specific conditions than you had envisioned. For other people, a formerly undetected medical issue, like vision or hearing issues, might be motivation enough to stop the preparation.

However, if the training works out and you and your dog become a treatment team, you can start visiting offices booked through your chosen association. This will be a definitive trial of your dog's conduct in actual pet therapy settings. After you get out there and begin having an effect, you'll be happy you invested your time and energy to go through the process of training, testing, and certifying. You and your well-prepared dog will wear your emotions on your faces, smiling broadly at the many people you will help by perking those up who need it most.

More Tips:

- Be sure to socialize your dog with many new individuals (both human and animal) by visiting many types of places that feature various items and surfaces for your pet to explore.

- Achieve the AKC Canine Good Citizen title for your dog. Train fundamental practices for treatment work, including "leave it," "watch me," free chain strolling, and not jumping up on people or "four on the floor."

- Consider raising the bar and working towards the AKC Advanced Canine Good Citizen (AKC Community Dog) title. For the best type of practice, rehearse items you will encounter on the CGC test in actual situations. If you live or plan to visit highly populated urban and metropolitan areas, visit online Urban CGC resources to browse specialized information.

- Enlist your dog in a treatment dog class that will successfully prepare you and your dog for visits. Many courses will incorporate a treatment dog assessment toward the end of the class to ensure you and your dog have what it takes to succeed in the field.

- Once you've breezed through your assessment, register with a public treatment dog association to start making visits and lighting up lives. Both before and after the exam, it's your obligation as a handler to steadily maintain your dog's training and good behavior to ensure they're the best treatment dog they can be.

Horse

THERAPY HORSES

Many people are surprised to learn that horses, often viewed only as farm workers, sport animals, or riding companions, can provide a great deal of emotional assistance. Horses are utilized in therapeutic settings to help clients traverse complex emotional events, in addition to the bond they have with their owners.

What Is Equine-Assisted Therapy?

Horses are used in the therapeutic process in what is referred to as equine-assisted psychotherapy. While under the supervision of a mental health professional, people participate in activities such as grooming, feeding, and leading a horse.

The main objectives of this type of treatment include assisting individuals in improving abilities such as establishing enthusiastic guidelines, improving self-assurance, and learning about responsibilities and obligations. With mature horses weighing anywhere from around 900 to 2,000 pounds or more, it may feel somewhat scary to have such a large, grand animal participating in your treatment meetings.

However, equine-assisted treatments are growing in popularity based on their experiential methodology and expanding proof of their adequacy. There is an assortment of terms used to depict or reference equine-assisted psychotherapy, including:

- Equine-assisted mental health
- Equine-assisted counseling
- Equine-facilitated psychotherapy
- Equine-assisted therapy

The last term, equine-assisted therapy, can likewise allude to different types of treatment where horses are utilized, for example, with spoken therapy treatment.

History of Equine Therapy

The idea of horses being used to heal is not particularly new. Instead, horses have been utilized for therapeutic purposes since the age of the ancient Greeks. The Greek doctor Hippocrates, known as the "Father of Medicine," expounded on the remedial capability of horseback riding.

Riding became better known as a treatment device during the 1950s and 1960s. In 1969, the North American Riding for Handicapped Association was formed, later becoming the Professional Association of Therapeutic Horsemanship (PATH) International.

Who Can Horses Help?

Equine-assisted psychotherapy (EAP) can be utilized with an assortment of populaces and in various settings. Indeed, horses can be used with individuals, families, and other groups. While equine-assisted psychotherapy is not ordinarily the only type of treatment, it can be a rather integral therapeutic aid that can be utilized in association with more standard treatment options.

Offering a vastly different encounter than customary treatments that involve simply talking, EAP brings individuals outside and offers a potential chance to utilize all faculties while exploring and managing inner challenges

Horses, Children, and Teens

Equine-assisted psychotherapy might be similarly viable as a treatment option for kids and youngsters as it is for adult patients. Similarly, as with adults, youths and adolescents can encounter injuries, uneasiness, sorrow, PTSD, and then some.

Equine treatment offers younger patients a remedial climate that can feel less compromising and significantly more welcoming than a conventional psychologist or other mental help professional's office. Most kids interested in EAP are between 6 to 18 years of age.

Kids frequently find it hard to open up and struggle to handle complicated feelings and emotions. Equine-assisted psychotherapy permits young people to pinpoint and work to improve emotional problems by:

- Increasing assertiveness
- Growing self-confidence
- Developing and maintaining relationships
- Improving emotional awareness
- Learning to show greater empathy
- Improving impulse control
- Developing problem-solving skills
- Attaining social skills
- Trusting in others
- Trusting in themselves

- Increasing adaptability
- Higher tolerance for distress
- More emotional awareness
- Greater independence
- Improved impulse control
- Higher self-esteem
- Greater social awareness
- Improved social relationships

The Benefits of Horses in the Practice of Pet Therapy

Horses have unique characteristics that have led to them becoming a top choice for animal-assisted therapies, even though several species can be employed in the psychotherapeutic process. Horses add the following distinctive features to the therapy process, according to anxiety expert Dr. Robin Zasio:

Non-Judgmental and Unbiased

Even though people, particularly therapists, strive to provide a secure environment to examine profound emotional traumas and unpleasant experiences, clients may find it difficult to discuss their thoughts openly. As participants work toward creating trust and exercising vulnerability in session, developing therapeutic rapport might take some time.

However, the horse's presence may provide a sense of calm because they will only react to the client's actions and emotions, with no threat of bias or judgment of their emotional experience.

Feedback and Mirroring

Horses are excellent observers, always on the lookout for movement and expression. They frequently mimic a client's actions or feelings, providing a sense of understanding and connection to make them feel secure. Additionally, clients can maintain a feeling of self-awareness by using the horse's behavior and interactions as feedback. This provides valuable opportunities for the client to check in and understand what's going on in the moment.

Managing Vulnerability

When clients are trying to open up about emotional issues, past experiences, or life transitions, they may feel exposed. The horse can provide a reference point for processing these feelings and emotions.

If something is too painful to talk about, clients may find it easier to process by using the horse as an example or aligning their experiences with the horse's experiences. Externalizing their inner emotions can help people approach and comprehend them more easily.

Horses, too, require effort. They must be fed, watered, exercised, and groomed regularly. It is often therapeutic to provide this type of attention. It aids in the establishment of routines and structure, and the act of caring for and nurturing another living being can assist in the development of empathy.

Conditions Equine-Assisted Therapy Can Treat

There is a growing body of evidence that backs up equine-assisted therapy's effectiveness in treating a variety of ailments, including:

Anxiety

Around 17 million people in the United States suffer from anxiety problems. Although most people experience anxiety at some point in their lives, especially when confronted with change or uncertainty, there are times when anxiety meets clinical diagnostic criteria. Anxiety disorders can include, but aren't limited to, the following:

- Agoraphobia
- Generalized anxiety disorder
- Panic disorder
- Separation anxiety
- Selective mutism
- Social anxiety disorder
- Specific phobia

Many individuals who battle high levels of nervousness wind up trapped in stress over their past and dread their future because of it. Dr. Zasio calls attention to the idea that working with a horse during the remedial cycle can provide freedom for customers to "remain present and zeroed in on the main job."

Since horses are cautious about their behavior and feelings, they can detect risk and react with increased mindfulness, which ordinarily prompts an adjustment of their behavior and leads them to move away. Customers who battle with uneasiness can connect with this capacity to detect danger signals and react similarly. Handling personal difficulties by exploring a horse's conduct can be more straightforward for specific individuals than speaking more straightforwardly about their own encounters with anxiety.

One more advantage of involving equine-assisted psychotherapy in the treatment of anxiety is that it assists individuals with rehearsing their weaknesses in a protected setting. As people figure out how to interface with the horse and attempt new things, they move out of their usual comfort zone with support from the therapist and the horse.

This enables the therapist to manage their experience and work to improve areas of stress and anxiety, including feelings of dread and difficulties handling new experiences. Additionally, the caregiver can point out any relevant observations, revelations, or triumphs in those minutes during treatment.

Post-Traumatic Stress Disorder

After a stressful experience, post-traumatic stress disorder (PTSD) can be severe, with heightened alertness and reactivity, intrusive memories and nightmares, and avoidance symptoms. According to the Anxiety and Depression Association of America (AADA), 7.7 million Americans aged 18 and up suffer from PTSD.

PTSD can affect children, teenagers, and adults. Although several traumatic events most frequently lead to the development of PTSD, including persons who have been sexually assaulted and veterans who have served in combat, it can be caused by a single event. These individuals have significantly greater rates of PTSD development.

The use of equine-assisted psychotherapy in treating post-traumatic stress disorder in veterans is on the rise. Tess Hassett, a riding instructor at the Northern Virginia Therapeutic Riding Program, has a clinical psychology background and uses EAP to help veterans daily.

In describing her work with soldiers, Hassett observed, "Many of them have stated that after their PTSD and despair, they never imagined they'd be able to bond with someone and have that personal connection again. They are, nevertheless, feeling that connection with their horse. They can apply this to the rest of their lives as well as their relationships."

Addiction Treatment

It is realized that the abuse of prescription medication, recreational drugs, and alcohol continues to rise to even more dangerous levels in the United States. The Center for Disease Control and Prevention (CDC) states that more than 70,000 individuals passed away from a medication overdose in 2017 alone.

Large numbers of these deaths were caused by the plague of narcotics impacting the nation, with just about 50,000 deaths directly connected to narcotic use. This is, literally, a plague of reliance on narcotics—prescribed or illegally obtained. There is a growing need for successful methods to treat this dependence, which is at a record-breaking high.

Fortunately, equine-assisted psychotherapy offers a unique and remarkable way to treat the habit and underlying—or co-occurring—mental conditions. A co-occurring disorder, which used to be alluded to as a double determination, portrays a battle with dependence with another underlying psychological wellness condition. This is typically the case in issues relating to addiction and substance abuse.

The most definitive objective of treatment for those suffering from addiction is to assist customers with living calm, sound, and valuable lives. Ordinarily, these customers are also in treatment to mend harmful relationship elements, for example, within their families or with their friends. Figuring out how to trust, show weakness, and healthily convey their feelings can be tested during equine-assisted therapy.

EAP can assist customers with figuring out how to foster a feeling of trust through their connections with the horse. As they gain a sense of wellbeing and develop a closer relationship, the experience can urge people to allow themselves to be helpless as they learn new things and cooperate with the horse. This will increase trust.

Attention-Deficit/Hyperactivity Disorders (ADD/ADHD)
Treating attention-deficit/hyperactivity issues (ADHD) is a treatment area where equine-assisted psychotherapy can be particularly helpful. Some report that EAP is especially valuable to both adults and youth with ADHD since it offers them a practical, fun, and involved way to obtain insight into the challenges they face.

The customer is ordinarily with a trained therapist, an equine expert, and the horse during equine-assisted treatment. Riding isn't typically associated with equine-assisted psychotherapy. Instead, the emphasis is on presence, consideration, care, limits, meaningful gestures, and that's only the tip of the iceberg.

Kay Trotter, Ph.D., an authorized proficient instructor, creator, and originator of Equine Partners in Counseling (EPIC) Enterprises, was one of the first to explore the viability of equine-assisted psychotherapy. Trotter observed that introducing horses to individuals with issues requiring remedial assistance greatly expanded positive practices while decreasing negative ones.

Her study was one of the first to be published on EAP viability. It was printed in the Journal for Creativity in Mental Health. It has been shown that customers can receive an assortment of benefits from equine-assisted psychotherapy, such as:

- Increased self-esteem
- Increased self-respect
- Improved adjustment to routines and guidelines
- Improved focus
- Less stressful friendships
- Reduced aggression

For people battling ADHD, the feelings of achievement brought on during an equine-assisted psychotherapy meeting can be of incredible advantage. As an authorized clinical social specialist, Kit Muellner reveals, "Customers feel that they've accomplished something all alone, rather than being told to accomplish something by a parent or instructor." It is truly an extraordinary experience for many of the individuals seeking treatment.

Muellner explains, "A 1,500-pound animal reacts how you need him to because you asked him to. So, by getting the horse to do as you wanted, you've achieved something you needed to do, as opposed to something that another person needed you to do." It is empowering for someone struggling with these challenges in their daily life.

This feeling of achievement can feel huge for anybody, particularly somebody who battles with ADHD. In those minutes, they are getting moment-to-moment constructive criticism from their horse while figuring out how to foster trust, convey their thoughts and desires viably, and learn to move forward with the next thing after achieving an individual objective.

Equine-Assisted Therapists

The Equine Assisted Growth and Learning Association (EAGALA) is a non-profit organization devoted to setting the norm for experts working with horses in a therapeutic setting. They have prepared and implemented a specific confirmation process for those wishing to take steps to become a respected, well-trained equine-assisted treatment provider.

Notwithstanding EAGALA, there are several different projects devoted to appropriately training equine-assisted therapists and supporting the establishment of norms for those working with customers in the field of EAP.

To become a treatment provider, you should contact your state administrative board whether you expect to be giving equine-assisted treatment or not. They will help you determine the instructive and clinical prerequisites you must complete to become authorized to do this type of work in your state. Equine-assisted treatment is a very specific specialization inside the field of psychotherapy, with clinicians acquiring extraordinary levels of training to provide EAP successfully.

People and animals form deep and critical bonds. These friendships can be particularly advantageous to people. Animals give us unrestricted empathy, persistence, and love—and honestly, to have a companion in an animal is a genuine gift. Research shows that possessing a pet can make us more joyful and provide a better outlook on life. Also, service animals can help the disabled to achieve more independence and tackle challenges like strolling down the road or adapting to and controlling anxiety.

Pets like dogs, cats, birds, and even horses have been utilized in clinical settings for upward of 150 years. Today, there's substantially more research backing up the advantages of the practice of pet-assisted treatments. Horses, specifically, can be incredible resources in our treatment endeavors, regardless of what diagnosis or challenges you're managing. Many sorts of individuals in different circumstances can benefit from pet treatment with horses, including:

Teens

Every teenager goes through a phase where they fight to be heard and for their feelings to be validated, yet they still feel misunderstood. However, some face more significant issues than others. Particularly at risk are those who struggle to convey how they feel or focus on misuse and abuse of substances as a crutch. They've developed such instruments to hold themselves back from feeling powerless.

Yet, horses can help to reveal the issues an adolescent may be encountering. Horses can assist teens with managing issues such as:

- Depression
- ADD and ADHD
- Mood disorders
- Addiction
- Communication challenges
- Trust issues
- Trauma and abuse

Pet therapy with horses isn't based on horseback riding. It can be part of the interaction, but face-to-face engagement and nonverbal communication are more critical components. A horse demands a calm demeanor, and the way it reacts to a teen's body language can help them comprehend their own emotions.

Seniors

Studies indicate that seniors who own pets live longer, better, and more joyful lives. Be that as it may, possessing a pet probably won't be practical for all seniors. Individuals living in nursing homes, senior living, or assisted-living facilities frequently can't have pets. Further, their medical issues can make it difficult to focus and care for an animal.

However, exposure to and interactions with pets can assist seniors with bringing down their heart rates and fending off loneliness and depression. So how might we help? Pet-assisted treatment is regularly an ideal choice for seniors needing a little animal friendship.

One miniature horse makes senior residents at a Michigan nursing office exceptionally glad. Charlie and his owner Ronica visit their neighborhood senior facility to spread grins and giggles. Charlie is a unique, pint-sized horse. Since he was brought up in close contact with people, he is remarkably manageable and loving. Indeed, he flourishes as the center of attention.

Recovering Addicts

Among the numerous ways horses can help individuals in their treatment endeavors, some are better aided than others.

For example, fixation recuperation treatments are benefitted significantly. Patients invest energy mingling and focusing on the horses, which helps construct trust, responsibility, self-esteem, and certainty.

Individuals recuperating from fixation frequently experience a decrease in their psychological and physical wellbeing. Pet treatment with horses involved can help these individuals lower their circulatory strain, lessen feelings of anxiety, and learn the importance of persistence.

Horses can be incorporated into pet therapy for a broad scope of individuals and mental and physical health challenges. Other animals can, as well. Assuming you have an extraordinary horse, consider electing to assist individuals battling issues like melancholy and addiction by sharing your companion. No one can say for sure, but your horse could change someone else's day-to-day existence for the better, similar to how it most likely changed yours.

Things to Consider

When considering equine-assisted therapy for yourself or a loved one, there are a few things to keep in mind. Always keep your physical ability and overall health as the priority. Before starting horse therapy, consult your doctor if you have scoliosis, spina bifida, or another spinal or back-related health concern.

Timing

The timing of EAP may or may not be suitable depending on the client's issues. When someone is struggling with addiction, for example, they will need time to detox and establish compliance with a treatment program before introducing equine-assisted therapy services.

Fear

Even though equine-assisted therapy has been proven effective in treating anxiety, a client may be afraid of being near a large horse and hence be unwilling to participate in this sort of treatment. There could also be a traumatic experience associated with animals that prevents someone from participating. Forcing someone to become involved would likely hinder, rather than help, the individual.

To find out if you or a loved one is a suitable fit for equine-assisted therapy, speak with a certified mental health professional. Before beginning any treatment, most programs will assess your needs to see if EAP is appropriate for you.

Cost

Because equine-assisted psychotherapy has only recently begun to gain popularity and momentum as an effective treatment for mental health and substance abuse, many insurance policies may not cover the costs associated with this service.

The cost of EAP services varies by location and can be rather expensive. It's a good idea to talk to your insurance provider and your local equine therapy institution ahead of time to iron out the technicalities and ensure it fits into your budget.

Why Horses?

- Horses are intuitive and sensitive animals.
- Human emotions are mirrored in horses.
- Between horses and humans, there is a strong bond.
- Horses provide unconditional love.
- Horses help people relax by accepting them and enabling them to give and take, which increases confidence and attention.

- Because of their modest stature, smaller horses and miniature horses provide a non-threatening therapy experience for children, elders, and those in wheelchairs.

Is Equine-Assisted Therapy Effective?

Faithful, cherished, and reliable, horses are animals people have quickly bonded with throughout history. Indeed, even the ancient Greeks saw how individuals appeared to act more calmy and express a demeanor of joy while interacting with a horse. Something about the delicate, patient nature of a horse triggers feelings of certainty and confidence in individuals who experience the ill effects of mental or genuinely crippling physical handicaps.

Horses are huge, strong animals, and they can frequently feel threatening to individuals who have little insight or experience being around them. Nonetheless, equine-assisted treatment is intended to assist individuals with defeating that underlying feeling of initial terror to foster a profound, enduring bond with the animal.

Equine-assisted therapy specialists think the imposing appearance of horses joined with their delicate and tolerating nature helps individuals achieve emotional wellness and substance recuperation. Through these non-intrusive treatment programs, individuals can find out a great deal about themselves while exploring the advantages of compassion and trust.

Horses additionally have particular—and unique—personalities that are vital for equine treatment patients to accomplish their program objectives. Like individual humans, horses can be outgoing, modest, somewhat obstinate, and friendly. Some are calm, and others can be rowdy. Some are downright silly. Nothing is more helpful than realizing you have a devoted, cherished companion who will welcome you consistently with tail washes, "nosings," and a profound craving for your companionship.

Horses are sensitive animals that promptly feel a connection with people they interact with every day or frequently. By responding to non-verbal communication and reflecting the dispositions of their guardians, horses make the ideal, non-judgmental "specialist" by using body language and non-verbal cues to offer a deep understanding of an individual's harmful practices and challenging emotions.

THE BEST THERAPY ANIMALS

Many individuals require a significant amount of assistance in various forms to accomplish their everyday responsibilities. Certain individuals can't live autonomously without several individuals and extraordinarily trained pets helping them through their life journey. Others, however, benefit greatly from an encounter with an animal that simply furnishes them with a feeling of calm and allows them to unwind. Treatment animals offer all of these levels of assistance based on physical needs and mental wellbeing.

Not to be mistaken for an emotional support dog or a service dog, treatment animals are well-socialized and carefully trained to provide solace and affection to individuals encountering many different distressing conditions. Treatment animals are usually found in clinics, nursing homes, schools, and war zones fall into one of three categories: remedial treatment animals, animal-assisted treatment animals, or office treatment animals.

The most widely recognized sort of treatment animal is an animal-assisted treatment animal. These are regular pets that travel to different locations to visit with individuals who might miss their own pets due to a forced separation. These animals, however, return home with their owners toward the day's end. A wide range of animals can be used as treatment animals. Regardless of the species, these animals must receive regular veterinary care and evaluation, fundamental training and preparation, and be screened to guarantee they interact well with many different types of individuals. Federal laws do not govern treatment animals; however, a few states have laws that allow certain freedoms to the owners and their pets. Vests, restraints, and various other goods are accessible through the National Service Animal Registry.

Therapy Dogs

By far the most commonly seen treatment animal, dogs come in all shapes and sizes and make ideal treatment animals. Most people have likely come across a treatment dog at some point throughout their life. Treatment dogs are regularly seen in emergency clinics, nursing homes, schools, prisons, and other unexpected places where you might be shocked to see a dog strolling around.

We all know that dogs make exemplary allies and companions to humans, so it is not at all unexpected that those who would otherwise be unable to interact with them long to be in their presence. Reviews have shown that dogs help quiet and calm individuals and the function of treatment dogs demonstrates this. Larger dog varieties, like Labradors and Golden Retrievers, are most frequently seen as treatment dogs, yet that doesn't mean that other types cannot become wonderful treatment animals. As long as a dog is agreeable towards individuals of all kinds and can be taught to follow obedience commands, it can most likely be turned into a treatment animal with the proper training and preparation!

Therapy Horses

Horses, while significantly larger than dogs, also make superb treatment animals. While you won't see a horse strolling through a school (unless it is a smaller breed, like a miniature horse), equine-assisted treatment methods use treatment horses to interact with individuals during treatment. Treatment horses are extraordinary animals who support psychological well-being. They are utilized in various therapies, including dependence therapy, veteran gatherings, and in conjunction with other mental health offices that clinical experts manage.

Directly interacting and engaging with a horse is frequently promoted as highly remedial. The often-mirrored human and horse emotions have been demonstrated to be exceptionally valuable for individuals dealing with a wide range of mental issues. Horses also help people develop emotional skills, including trust-building, exploring a hard-working attitude, and more effectively managing their feelings. While treatment horses may be ridden in therapy, it is not always the case. It may be beneficial to incorporate this feature into some types of treatment and not others, depending on the therapy objectives and the person's level of comfort with the animal.

Therapy Cats

Many cats may make excellent therapy animals, albeit they are seen somewhat less often than dogs or horses. Cats, like dogs, are easy to bring into indoor facilities like nursing homes and hospitals to help people who are missing their pets feel better. Many therapy cats are trained to walk on a leash and can provide a calming presence for children in schools, the elderly in assisted care homes, and others. They're also an excellent indoor therapy animal for those who are afraid of dogs.

Therapy Rabbits

A rabbit makes an excellent therapy animal when a tiny, quiet therapy animal is required. Rabbits are easy to transport, do not bark or meow, and are a perfect choice for people who are afraid of both dogs and cats, as a rabbit fear is uncommon.

A good therapy rabbit will be calm, well-socialized, and enjoy being handled and petted. It's good if a therapy rabbit can also use a litter box. Not all rabbits are suitable as therapy animals, but if a friendly bunny is at ease in a harness and on a four-foot leash, they could be an excellent choice.

WHAT DO WE RECEIVE BY GIVING MORE TO ANIMALS?

Animals help people in countless ways, from providing services (as guide dogs for the visually impaired or as treatment dogs) to offering us love and friendship in our day-to-day routines. Various research and studies have shown the beneficial influences animals have on people's physical and emotional well-being, which can be valued and utilized in numerous ways. Along these lines, we must offer something back to our animals—and perhaps the ideal way to do so is to dramatically improve an animal's day-to-day existence by adopting a pet from an animal shelter or rescue.

Whether they are dogs, cats, guinea pigs, monkeys, llamas, pigs, or hens, animals are of great benefit to humans. They frequently make a significant contribution to human wellbeing and recovery by performing a significant job, for instance, in treatment and recovery programs. They positively affect physical and psychological wellness, give us everyday reassurance, assist detainees with acclimating to life outside of prison, and can simply act as a quiet anchor during periods of upsetting circumstances. Animals lessen the anxiety owners feel during life challenges; they guide the visually impaired;

they caution those at risk for diabetic or epileptic fits. Animals are our perfect partners, aides, and companions—and for that, we owe them a great deal.

To keep up with or further develop their wellbeing, individuals are in some cases advised (contingent upon individual conditions) to embrace an animal. Trademarks like 'Recover, get a dog' are not just strong marketing, but they depend on genuine science. For instance, a new Czech study, Kardiozive Brno 2030, surveyed 1,700 individuals and determined that animal people (particularly dog owners) are more grounded than non-animal people. The review looked at the soundness of the cardiovascular arrangement of dog owners with non-dog owners. The co-creator of the study stated that dog owners were, by and large, more active and dynamic than their dog-less partners. Moreover, they ate better and had a superior glucose level.

FOUR PAWS' Animal Assisted Intervention program demonstrates that previously lost or abandoned dogs can be a tremendous resource for the general public. They are chosen, trained, and guaranteed by specialists to become effective treatment dogs. This program exists for the benefit of dog adopters, the individuals requiring treatment, and the animals who need a home.

Animals Help Us – Let Us Help Animals

We should already be well aware of our obligation towards our perfect partners, companions, and aides—our pets. This obligation doesn't just incorporate meeting the survival requirements of the animals every single day. It additionally implies putting time and effort into making a carefully considered choice of pet that fits in with your life. By taking on an animal, you are making a promise to provide a permanent home for them. Shelters are overwhelmed with an extraordinary number of pets who are desperate for homes.

In the United States alone, around 6.5 million animals are taken to animal shelters every year, and only 3.2 million are adopted into permanent homes. In 2017, 18,385 animals were taken into Swiss shelters, and only 12,123 animals were adopted. German animal shelters receive an influx of more than 300,000 dogs, cats, small vertebrates, birds, and other animals consistently—with only 100,000 pets adopted back out.

How Do Pets Make Us Feel Better?

Pets are indeed the things that make us the happiest (even happier than cake, which we adore). All day, every day, our hearts beat for all types of pets and their gorgeous paws and adorable faces. The companionship provided by a pet is an excellent approach to relieving anxiety and stress.

They're always there for you.

There's one face that always greets you when you return home, no matter who else comes into or out of your life. Your pet will be there for you through thick and thin, no matter what. They'll be your cuddling buddy when you've had a terrible day or your binge TV buddy while you're watching Netflix late at night. For the rest of the animal's life, you'll have a friend by your side when you have a pet.

They keep you active.

One of the most pleasing aspects of owning a pet is, quite simply, you're compelled to use your legs more often! With an active pet, you can say goodbye to the couch-potato lifestyle and welcome the fresh air and sunshine. Running after your pet does count as cardio.

Pets can reduce your stress levels.

This is something science says, not us. According to studies, having a pet makes it easier to deal with stressful situations. Playing with your pet releases feel-good chemicals in your brain like dopamine and oxytocin, which trigger feelings of pleasure and happiness. Stroking your pet can help lower your blood pressure.

They are the ultimate source of comfort.

Do you have too many files on your desk? Is it possible that your favorite dress will no longer fit you? A hug or nuzzle from your pet will brighten your day faster than the sunlight in the morning.

Pets are a constant source of entertainment.

Keep it handy and start filming your pets using your camera. With their entertaining antics, pets contribute to some of the best home films, and you'll never get tired of watching their curiosity shine!

HOW TO FIND THE PERFECT PET

Congratulations! If, after reading this book, you've decided that keeping a pet is the correct choice for you: you're about to embark on a unique and rewarding relationship. While having a pet makes people happier, more independent, and more secure than those who don't, it's crucial to choose the right pet for your living conditions and lifestyle.

Discuss your preferences for a pet with the rest of your family and develop a list of attributes you like and those you'd rather avoid. Man's best friend, dogs come in various breeds and mixes, each with its own set of personality traits and specific needs. One dog breed may be perfect for one family but not work for another.

If you want something smaller and less energetic, a cat or rabbit may be the appropriate choice for you and your family. When hunting for the ideal pet, consider the following questions:

- **Living Space:** Do you have a backyard or live in a tiny apartment? This will significantly impact the size of the animal that is most suited to your home. A cat or a caged animal, for example, may be more acceptable for apartment life than a giant dog or a breed that needs a great deal of exercise.

- **Level of Attention:** How much of each day will the animal be alone? If you're going to be gone for the majority of the day and don't plan on hiring a pet sitter or using a pet daycare, you'll want an animal that doesn't require a lot of attention, rather than a dog.

- **Pet Size Considerations:** Do you have small children or someone fragile or disabled who may be knocked over by a large dog or a rambunctious puppy? Perhaps a smaller animal would be a better choice.

- **Shedding and Grooming:** How much shedding are you willing to put up with? Dogs and cats shed—and many breeds require grooming at regular intervals. You may choose a pet that doesn't shed at all, like an iguana or a snake, if you want a pet that sheds less—at least its hair!

- **Affordability:** How much money do you have for vet's bills, insurance, food, toys, etc.? Some charities offer low-cost veterinary care, but they are limited to certain areas, and you must meet specific financial criteria.

The most important part of selecting your pet is being completely honest with yourself about your lifestyle and the type of pet you'd like to add to your family. Start small, perhaps with a fish or a smaller, confined animal if you're unsure about caring for a larger animal. Check it out to see how it fits your life and go from there.

Shelter and Rescue Animals

Whether mixed breed or purebred, dogs, cats, and other animals acquired from a shelter or rescue group can make terrific pets. Most of the time, animals wind up in shelters due to no fault of their own. Their owner may have died or relocated to an area where pets are not permitted, or the pet may simply have been abandoned by irresponsible owners who acquired them on a whim. Far too often, people learn that they are unable (or unwilling) to care for their pets far too late, which is one of the reasons it is crucial to put extensive thought into what animal will work for you. If an animal at a shelter or rescue group shows hostile behavior, it is usually euthanized rather than being put up for adoption. Further, many shelters list the type of families that would best match individual pets (i.e., no children, no cats, etc.).

Rescue organizations work to find homes for unwanted or abandoned dogs, cats, and other pets. Many are seized from "high kill" shelters where they would have been euthanized. The animals are generally cared for by volunteers and often placed in "foster" homes until a permanent home is found. As a result, rescuers are frequently intimately aware of a pet's temperament and may advise you on whether a pet would be a suitable fit for your requirements.

You will not only be giving a home to a worthy pet and receiving many benefits in return, but you will also be saving an animal's life if you adopt from a shelter or rescue organization.

Alternatives to Pet Ownership

There are other methods of reaping the many health advantages of being around animals, even if you don't have the time, money, or capacity to keep a pet full-time. You may, for example, ask to walk a neighbor's dog or volunteer at an animal shelter. Volunteers are often invited to help care for homeless dogs, work on training efforts, socialize cats, or assist at adoption events. You'll be helping not just yourself but also the animals through these interactions, which make them more adoptable and comfortable around a wide variety of types of people.

Pet "rental" programs are available at several animal shelters and rescue organizations. Adoptable dogs and cats can be taken for walks or played with regularly. You can also temporarily foster an animal until a permanent home can be found—or until you determine whether the animal is suited for you. Some shelters even have special foster promotions for their elderly pets—they will handle the medical bills if you provide the dog a happy, safe place for the remainder of its life. This is helpful because many people cannot take on the extra expense of caring for an older pet. Still, it would otherwise be an excellent match and will provide the animal with peace and tranquility during its golden years.

Specially trained therapy dogs and cats are available from several groups as well. These animals visit children's hospitals, assisted living institutions, nursing homes, hospice programs, shelters, and schools. People are given the opportunity to pet and brush the animals during these visits, boosting mood and reducing tension and anxiety. Many of the people in these facilities were forced to leave beloved pets behind when they could no longer care for them, so this provides a much-needed opportunity to fill that void in some way.

Or, contact a local animal shelter to see what volunteer opportunities they might have available. They might require volunteers to exercise, care for, and socialize animals. You could consider fostering an animal assuming that you're ready to have a pet temporarily but can't afford long-term veterinary bills or commit to permanent adoption. Many shelter animals are timid and fearful in the shelter environment. They require the harmony and calm of someone's home while waiting to find their permanent families.

CONCLUSION

Throughout this book, I've not been referring to animals that have been trained to obey commands; instead, I'm referring to the dogs, cats, and any other domesticated animal that we encounter daily. Contact with an animal, such as petting, feeding, and chatting to a pet, provides a sense of pleasure, tranquility, and joy, which aids in therapies and treatments for children and adults. Dramatic healing can occur through fearless physical interaction with animals and the environment. Children believe that the animal needs them, and therefore they feel a boost in self-esteem and mental wellbeing.

Animal-assisted therapy is not an elective medication strategy but rather an alternate way to deal with mental issues that have been used for generations in one way or another. The ancient Greeks accepted that dogs could help people recuperate from diseases and welcomed their presence in their healing sanctuaries. Working with pets had its beginnings in 1792 in England, where the doctor William Tuke utilized dogs to improve the day-to-day living environment of patients in hospitals. In 1867, in Germany, dogs were used to provide epileptic treatment. In 1944, the Red Cross in New York involved dogs in their recovery efforts of soldiers. Internationally, there are countless programs where dogs are utilized in either ongoing or short-term work, aiding the recovery of patients.

As previously mentioned, the ancient Greeks used dogs in medicine. Asclepius, the God of Medication and Healing, was said to have increased healing and recovery through blessed dogs. Alternative medication considers turtles and different reptiles as key components for healing certain afflictions. The many positive impacts that horses have on individuals with mental or physical issues are additionally well-documented.

Today, more and more studies indicate that animal-assisted treatment is becoming more linked to concrete science. Rupert Sheldrake, in his book Dogs That Know When Their Owners Come Home and Other Unexplained Powers of Animals, indicates that at this time, there are more than 2,000 projects in the U.S. alone, in which animals visit individuals in emergency clinics, hospices, and nursing homes. For the most part, these animals are pets who live with volunteers and are frequently called PAT (pet as treatment) animals. Furthermore, some individuals visit and allow their dogs and cats to interact with burnt-out, discouraged, or forlorn individuals. Likewise, different animals are valuable, including birds, turtles, rabbits, and even fish.

Hundreds of stories about animals that comfort and heal are included in his book, most of which concern cats and dogs who improve the lives of sick or sad people. I invite you, my readers, to start your own story by adopting or fostering an animal need. The rewards for both you and your pet are evidenced in these pages. Adopting a dog, cat, horse, or other animals can change lives – yours and your new pets – for the better!

If you enjoyed this title and would like to read about other topics that have changed my life, please check out my new books on Amazon or my website: www.my-mindguide.com.

Also, let's stay connected on social media. Please drop a line on Facebook or Instagram, and stay tuned for updates! You're welcome to share your thoughts with me directly as well: gassner@my-mindguide.com. In return, I'll send you a gorgeous infographic that you can cut out and frame.

Also, please leave a review on Amazon, as this will help me to reach an even broader audience. Thank you so much for your time, insight, and undying hunger for knowledge!

I want to say thank you to all of my colleagues, clients, friends, and family members, who have all contributed to what I am now.

I also want to say thank you to Gabriel Palacios, the king of hypnotherapy and a Swiss bestseller author who taught this old fox new tricks, letting me deep-dive into the mystery of hypnotherapy. I learned so much along the journey that I'm now a certified master-hypnosis coach and conversation coach myself!

Furthermore, I want to say thank you to the fantastic teachers of SAMYANA/Bali who trained me to become a certified yoga and meditation teacher.

Last but not least, I give a special thanks to my master-teacher Eckhard Wunderle, who's close to a saint to me. He introduced me to the world of meditation and let me discover all the wonders it has to offer. I couldn't be more proud about having received my certification as a meditation teacher from directly from him at the Institut für Spirituelle Psychologie.

Peace, love, and happiness to all of you—till next time!

Authors portrait

Kurt Friedrich Gassner has worn many hats throughout his lifetime, including but not limited to serial entrepreneur, Creative Director, Meditation Teacher, Licensed Hypnotherapist, and more recently, self-improvement author. Leveraging his treasure trove of experiences and in-depth knowledge of psychology, he provides his readers with the tools they need to unlock their infinite potential.

As a prolific self-help writer, Kurt has authored the following books: *The Art of Forgiveness, Lie or Die, Soul-Match, Can You Inherit a Poisoned Mind?* and *The Power of Poverty*. He also authored a best-selling children's book in German-speaking countries and has over 20 books underway.

When it comes to enduring success, Kurt understands that financial prosperity isn't the only aspect one should strive for. He may be a self-made millionaire, but what really transformed his life is mastering his unconscious mind. Perseverance, personal power, self-awareness, and learning from past mistakes have all been key ingredients to bringing his dreams to fruition—and he strives to impart that wisdom onto others through his writing.

During his spare time, Kurt Friedrich Gassner is either traveling across the globe, golfing, biking in the Alps, hiking, or spending quality time with his loved ones. For the last 37 years, he has been happily married and he is the father of two successful children. Presently, he resides in both Munich, Germany, and Kirchberg, Austria.

OTHER BOOKS BY THE AUTHOR

My-mindguide.com
GROW
WITH YOUR
FAILURES
GROW THROUGH YOUR FAILURES
KURT GASSNER

My-mindguide.com
WACHSE
MIT DEINEN
MISSERFOLGEN
WACHSE DURCH DEINE MISSERFOLGE
KURT GASSNER

My-mindguide.com
Lass
Los!
Verändere dein Unter- Bewusstsein, befreie dich
von materieller Abhängigkeit & wahre Lebensgeschichten
KURT GASSNER

My-mindguide.com
Let
Go
Rewire your subconscious mind with hypnosis
& cure material addiction – Real Life Stories
KURT GASSNER

My-mindguide.com
NEVER APPLIED
THE ULTIMATE POWER TO THINK AND ACT OUT OF THE BOX
KURT GASSNER

My-mindguide.com
NIEMALS BEWORBEN
DER ULTIMATIVE SCHLÜSSEL ZU UNKONVENTIONELLEM DENKEN
KURT GASSNER

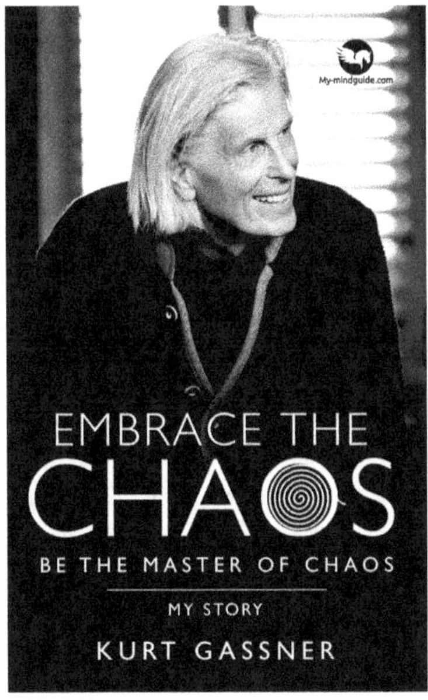

My-mindguide.com
EMBRACE THE CHAOS
BE THE MASTER OF CHAOS
MY STORY
KURT GASSNER

My-mindguide.com
DAS CHAOS BEHERRSCHEN
WERDE MEISTER DES CHAOS
MEINE GESCHICHTE
KURT GASSNER

ECKO
FIRED FOR SUCCESS?
TRUE STORIES AND MANAGEMENT LESSONS
FOR OUR TOUGH CHANGING TIMES
KURT GASSNER

ECKO
WEGEN ERFOLG GEFEUERT
Eine wahre Geschichte über das Scheitern in Unternehmen und
was junge Führungskräfte aus einer Fehlerkultur lernen können.
KURT GASSNER

My-mindguide.com
Unlocking
The Healing
Power of Pets
What Pets Can Tell You About Your Soul
KURT GASSNER

My-mindguide.com
Heilkraft
Unserer
Lieblinge
Was Haustiere über Ihre Seele verraten können
KURT GASSNER

My-mindguide.com
THE
BLISS OF
STRUGGLE
WINNING STRATEGIES
FOR DEMANDING TIMES
KURT GASSNER

My-mindguide.com
STARK
DURCH
„STRUGGLES"
DAS IDEALE MINDSET,
UM KRISEN ZU MEISTERN
KURT GASSNER

My-mindguide.com
LIE LYING
& LIAR
A LIE HAS NO LEGS BUT IT HAS WINGS
KURT GASSNER

My-mindguide.com
LÜGE LÜGEN
& LÜGNER
EINE LÜGE HAT KEINE BEINE, ABER SIE HAT FLÜGEL
KURT GASSNER

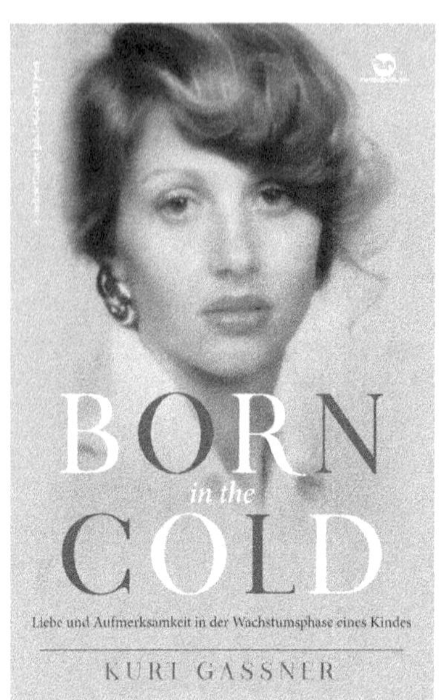

BORN
in the
COLD
Liebe und Aufmerksamkeit in der Wachstumsphase eines Kindes
KURT GASSNER

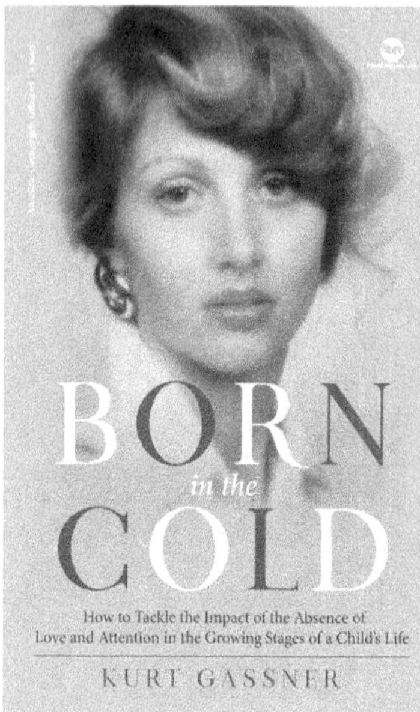

BORN
in the
COLD
How to Tackle the Impact of the Absence of
Love and Attention in the Growing Stages of a Child's Life
KURT GASSNER

SOPHIAS WUNDERWELT
10 ERZÄHLUNGEN
KURT GASSNER

SOPHIA'S WONDERWORLD
10 TALES
KURT GASSNER

BESTSELLING AUTHOR OF
The Art Of
FORGIVNESS
AMAZON #1 BESTSELLER
My-mindguide.com
A practical guide for self healing and overcome past traumas
The Art Of
FORGIVNESS
KURT GASSNER
My-mindguide.com
The Art Of
FORGIVNESS
KURT GASSNER